D0893770

AUSTRIA

TITLES IN THE MODERN NATIONS OF THE WORLD SERIES INCLUDE:

Austria
Brazil
Canada
China
Cuba
Egypt
England
Ethiopia
Germany
Greece
Haiti
India
Ireland
Italy
Japan
Jordan
Kenya
Mexico
Poland
Russia
Saudi Arabia
Scotland
Somalia
South Africa
South Korea
Spain
Sweden
Switzerland
Taiwan
The United States
Vietnam

AUSTRIA

BY ANNE AKE

LUCENT BOOKS
P.O. BOX 289011
SAN DIEGO, CA 92198-9011

On Cover: View of Salzburg

The author would like to thank Stefan Tissot for his excellent help with information and for much time devoted to serving as tour guide, translator, and, of course, good friend.

Library of Congress Cataloging-in-Publication Data

Ake, Anne, 1943–
    Austria / by Anne Ake.
        p. cm. — (Modern nations of the world)
    Includes bibliographical references and index.
    ISBN 1-56006-758-6 (alk. paper)
    1. Austria—Juvenile literature. [1. Austria.] I. Title. II. Series.
    DB17 .A29 2001
    943.6—dc21

                                                    00-010558

Copyright © 2001 by Lucent Books, Inc.
P.O. Box 289011, San Diego, CA 92198-9011
Printed in the U.S.A.

CONTENTS

INTRODUCTION
A LAND OF CONTRADICTIONS

In 1996 Austria celebrated one thousand years of recorded history. Thousands of years earlier, before records were kept, people already lived in the land. As reminders of their life there, they left behind only a few graves, tools, and stone implements. Stone Age tribes—Celts, Magyars, and Goths among others—found their way into the land that is now Austria. Crusaders passed through and built churches along the way. Romans established communities and trading routes. Ottoman Turks fought for dominance of the strategically placed bit of land. All made their mark on the country's future. With thousands of years of multicultural history behind it, Austria is a land of contradictions.

A land that has known power, wealth, and grandeur, it has also seen abject poverty and political chaos. It has been ruled by archdukes, emperors, dictators, and a democracy of the people. The streets of Vienna have been traveled by bejeweled royalty in elegant carriages and by jackbooted storm troopers and military vehicles.

For centuries, life in Austria centered around the doctrines of the Catholic Church, yet it was the birthplace of the Protestant Reformation. After fighting bitterly for the right to be Protestant, its people reverted once again to Catholicism. Although Austria gained from the Reformation a respect for religious freedom, in the 1930s it built twenty-one concentration camps to torture and murder its Jewish population.

It is a land where the soaring towers and ornate architecture of opulent cathedrals are reflected in the glass and steel faces of twentieth-century office buildings. Powerful religious art exists side by side with the curves and sexual themes of the artists of the late 1800s. It is known for being the source of much of the world's most revered classical music, as well as the birthplace of one of the world's most hated dictators—Adolf Hitler.

Austria is also an international playground—a land of stunning beauty, of mountains, lakes, alpine pastures, and charming architecture. However, it struggles with pollution and eroding ecosystems. It is a nation of superhighways, and one where farmers must travel difficult mountain trails to take their herds to summer pasture. It is a country where ancient buildings have survived fire and war only to crumble under the patter of acid rain.

Austrian analyst Anton Pelinka wrote

Austria is not the same Austria it used to be: It is neither the Austria of the Habsburgs nor the Austria that was part of Nazi Germany. Nor is it the same Austria that came into existence when the Second Republic [the new government] was founded in 1945. The realities of present-day Austria are different from those of the past.[1]

Thousands of years of contradiction, controversy, and incongruity have created a modern nation that is strong, lively,

Austria, with its ornate architecture and stunning natural areas, is one of the world's most beautiful countries.

Austria is a land of contrasting political views, artistic styles, and geographic landscapes.

and sophisticated. Its cosmopolitan worldly population enjoys a high standard of living and a prominent position in the European community. Austrians revere their rich past and face the future with a wry and uniquely Austrian sense of humor.

A Cultural Mosaic

Fourteenth-century troubadours, wandering poets who entertained people with their poetry and music, described Austria as the fairest land on earth. The scenic beauty that once inspired these poet musicians to sing the praises of Austria still evokes similar responses today. The country, once the center of Europe's largest and most powerful empire, enters the twenty-first century with only 32,368 square miles of territory (about twice the size of Switzerland and slightly smaller than the state of Maine). However, its remaining land is so beautiful that many still consider it the crown jewel of Europe. More than 70 percent of Austria's land area is mountainous—rising from the rolling hills of the Vienna woods to the soaring snow-capped peaks of the Alps. Hundreds of rivers wind through the mountains and collect in the valleys to form countless lakes. Vineyards and orchards carpet fertile valleys and hillsides. Ornate public buildings and charming mountain chalets decorate cities and villages.

Eight other countries border this small landlocked nation: the Czech Republic, Germany, Hungary, Italy, Liechtenstein, Slovakia, Slovenia, and Switzerland. These close neighbors and the other cultures that have influenced the course of Austrian history left their mark on the land and the character of the people. Their influence is still apparent today and is one factor that gives each of the nine Austrian provinces its own ethnic heritage and individuality.

Lower Austria (Niederosterreich)

Austria's largest province, Lower Austria, is perched right at the top of the country—leading to some confusion over its name. The name comes from the province's location in the lower Danube River basin, not from its geographical position in the northeast. The Danube, the only major European river that flows eastward, flows out of southwest Germany through Upper Austria and on through Lower Austria on its way to the

Black Sea. It is understandable that the province should take its name from its relationship to the famed Danube, for the river has defined Lower Austria's place in history.

The Danube River valley forms an open thoroughfare for both water and land traffic to travel east and west across Europe through otherwise rugged mountain terrain. Countless travelers, settlers, and invaders found their way to Lower Austria, where many of them clashed, left their mark, and traveled on. Centuries of conflict have beset Austria, and much of it has taken place in this region. The dominant people of each era responded to the constant threat of invasion by building huge fortified castles and abbeys to protect their land and people.

Through the ages, more than a thousand castles were built and more than five hundred of them still stand today. Protective natural waterways or man-made moats surround many; others are perched high on rocky slopes. In days gone by, these castles were forbidding fortifications warding off invaders. Today they beckon foreign tourists.

Picturesque castles are not Lower Austria's only draw, however. The province's many forests such as the Wienerwald (Vienna Woods) are popular for hiking and other outdoor sports. And the much-touted benefits of hot underground springs that form natural thermal baths draw travelers from around the world to bask in their restorative waters. The village of Baden, in particular, has an international reputation for its thermal baths.

Besides a lively tourist business, Lower Austria has abundant natural resources, and much of the nation's industry is located here. Power plants, oil fields, refineries, textile and foodstuff factories, and steel and chemical plants produce many goods used throughout Austria. Much of the land of Lower Austria is relatively flat and fertile, and more land is under cultivation in this area than in any other province. According to the Austrian Press and Information Service, "[Lower Austria] is the country's biggest supplier of many agricultural products such as wheat and beet sugar, and . . . choice Austrian wines."[2]

Since 1986, the capital of Lower Austria has been the ancient city of St. Polten. St. Polten was settled under the name of Aelium Cetium by the Romans. The town almost disappeared after the departure of the Romans, but was later rebuilt and re-named. Its municipal charter, the document establishing it as a city, was granted in 1159 and is the oldest in Austria.

Upper Austria (Oberosterreich)

Lower Austria is linked to its neighboring province, Upper Austria, by the Danube and by the shared history of travelers who followed the path of the river. Upper Austria reveals even greater evidence of ties to the distant past. For instance, the village of Hallstatt dates back forty-five hundred years. Archaeologists believe it is the oldest settlement in Austria. The huge salt deposits, which are still mined today, probably attracted the first settlers to the shores of Hallstatter Lake. Early settlers used salt to preserve food for the long winters and traded it for other things they needed. Life centered around the salt mines, and archaeologists can trace the history of Hallstatt through two thousand graves, some from as early as 1000 B.C., that have been found near the mine entrance.

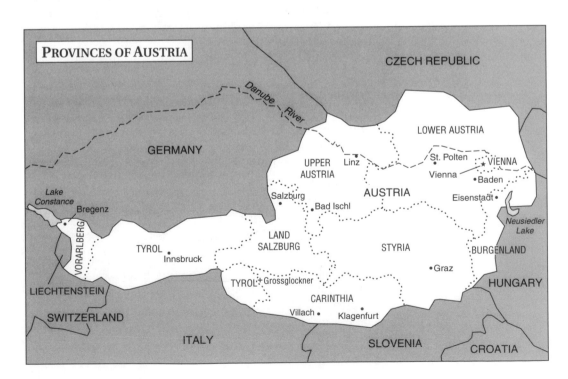

The ancient settlers built their homes on timbers set into the lake bottom, and many buildings in present-day Hallstatt still rest on these pilings. Today the old structures overhanging scenic Hallstatter Lake are very picturesque, and the village has become a favorite for day-trippers. Much of Upper Austria, including Hallstatt, is located in the Salzkammergut region, which many consider to be the most beautiful area in Austria.

Linz, the provincial capital, is a few miles north of the Salzkammergut region. Located on the important shipping route of the Danube, Linz is the third largest city in Austria. It is an industrial city with a skyline defined by smokestacks from steel works and chemical plants. The city's old town, however, presents a different ambiance with its picturesque old buildings, including the castle built by Emperor Frederick III in the 1400s.

SALZBURG

To the west of Upper Austria lies Land Salzburg. The province is called Land Salzburg to distinguish it from its capital, the city of Salzburg. Many people think the city, nestled into a landscape of breathtaking mountain scenery, is one of the world's most beautiful cities. Most visits to Salzburg include the ancient fortress Festung Hohensalzburg, which sits on a hill over-

WHITE GOLD

Salt has been so important to the prosperity of the Salzkammergut region of Austria that it has often been called "white gold," and place names in the area attest to the importance of the precious mineral. The German word *salz* means salt and is heard in Salzburg, Salzkammergut, and the Salzach River. In the ancient Celtic language the word for salt was *hall* and it too lingers on in village names such as Hallstatt, Hallein, and Hall.

Salt mines at Bad Ischl, Altausee, and Hallstatt are still in operation. Water in the mine causes the salt to dissolve and accumulate as brine or water with a heavy salt content. It takes ten to fifteen years for the brine in each new section of a mine to reach the height and saturation level to make pumping it out worthwhile. Once it has been pumped out, the brine is shipped to Ebensee in Upper Austria where the salt is extracted. Approximately 10 percent of the salt winds up as table salt; the rest is put to industrial use.

Because of its breathtaking mountain scenery, the city of Salzburg is believed by some to be the most beautiful city in the world.

looking the city. Today tourists flock up the mountain on foot or by cable car to visit the impressive staterooms and grisly torture chambers and to enjoy a magnificent view of the city and its surrounding countryside.

In early days, Salzburg was rich in many minerals, including salt, gold, arsenic, copper, and precious stones. With the exception of salt and copper, those resources are mostly gone now.

Today tourism is a mainstay of the economy, and even some of the oldest salt mines have become popular tourist attractions. For instance, at the mine at Durrnberg, first worked by the Celts, tourists can toboggan downhill along a chute of polished tree trunks, cross an underground salt lake on a raft, and ride in a miner's truck through long tunnels for a miner's eye view of salt mining. Additionally, beautiful scenery, ski slopes, and the lakes of the Salzkammergut make Land Salzburg popular with tourists year round.

Tyrol

East of Salzburg the country narrows into a corridor between Germany and Italy that is only between thirty-two and sixty kilometers (nineteen to thirty-two miles) wide. The first part of this mountainous strip is the province of Tyrol. Perhaps the world's most popular playground, Tyrol is sometimes called land of the mountains. Austria's third largest province, it is characterized by majestic slopes with beautiful meadows in the valleys in between.

Caring for tourists from all over the world is the most important industry in Tyrol—so much so that its other economic assets (namely its production of hydroelectric power) are sometimes overlooked. An information sheet from the Austrian Press and Information Service states: "Tyrol does indeed earn more foreign currency from tourism than any other province, but it [Tyrol] is also important for the production of hydroelectric power. It supplies areas of southern Germany with electricity, thus playing an important economic role in overall European terms."[3] Tyrol also produces other important products such as diesel engines, vehicles, glass gems, and optical glass used for high-quality lenses. The province is also well known for its traditional crafts such as Tyrolean embroidery and exquisite hand-cut crystal and mouth-blown glass.

The Goldene Dachl in Tyrol (shown here), built for the Emperor Maximilian I, featured a large ornate window so the emperor could watch street performances.

The great beauty of the area made Tyrol and particularly its capital, Innsbruck, popular with Austria's ruling classes. Royals such as Emperor Maximilian I, Archduke Ferdinand II, and Empress Maria Theresa all played a part in building the city. In the old city, examples of ornate architecture representing a variety of historic styles guard narrow winding cobblestone streets. The Goldenes Dachl (Golden Roof), which takes its name from the brilliance of the 2,657 copper tiles that cover its roof, is one such landmark. Built as a residence for Emperor Maximilian I, the Goldenes Dachl features a large window built out from the wall where the emperor sat to watch street performances.

In spite of its fine art and architecture, Innsbruck is best known for winter sports, particularly skiing. World attention focused on the city in 1964 and again in 1976 when the city hosted the Winter Olympics.

Tyrol was once much larger, but after World War I the Austrians lost the southern part to Italy. As a result Tyrol was almost ripped into two pieces. An area in the southeast is now attached to the rest of Tyrol by a narrow strip of rugged mountain terrain. Travel is almost impossible in this narrow, mountainous strip, making it necessary to go through Italy to reach this section of Austria's Tyrol province. However, this is not a major problem for the Tyrolean people because they still feel a close kinship with their southern neighbors who are now Italian citizens.

VORARLBERG

The Arlberg Alps separate the Tyrol from Vorarlberg, Austria's second smallest province. The mountains themselves, however, do not present a dramatic border because both provinces are almost completely covered by mountains. Vorarlberg and the Tyrol also share a thriving winter tourist business, and the Arlberg mountain range has an international reputation as a skiing center.

Lake Constance (also called Bodensee) on the northern border of Vorarlberg is a popular holiday resort area for European tourists. Vorarlberg shares the lake with Germany and Switzerland, and boat trips around the lake stop in all three countries.

Bregenz, the provincial capital, is located on the Bodensee and is best known for its annual music festival. The festival features international theatrical and musical productions performed on the Seebuhne, a large open-air floating stage at the edge of the lake.

The people of Vorarlberg share much of their heritage with their Swiss neighbors, so much so that even their language differs from the rest of Austria. Vorarlbergers speak a dialect of German that is more like Swiss-German than standard German. The language dates to Germanic Alemanni tribes who settled the region during the fifth century. As a result of those ties, Vorarlbergers feel a strong bond with the Swiss.

Like the Tyrol, Vorarlberg is best known for its appeal to tourists. Yet the province's production of hydroelectric power and textiles also makes an important contribution to the Austrian economy and provides power to Germany, Belgium, the Netherlands, and Luxembourg.

Grossglockner mountain lies within the province of Carinthia and is a popular hiking area.

CARINTHIA (KARNTEN)

The province of Carinthia is located east of Tyrol on the southern edge of Austria. In a land known for towering mountains, this province boasts the highest in the country—Grossglockner, with an elevation of 3,797 meters (12,457 feet). Mountain climbing is a popular sport in Carinthia, and several mountain climbing schools are located in the province. Fertile green valleys and more than twelve hundred mountain lakes make Carinthia popular with hikers and water sports enthusiasts year round.

Carinthia is ringed by tall mountains with only a few narrow passes allowing entrance to travelers from the rest of the world. Over the centuries, many people found their way through these passes to settle in the green valleys on the other side. They left the tale of their journey recorded in ruins and artifacts. Stone Age people came, followed by Celts, Romans, Slovenians, and finally German-speaking peoples. In the southern part of the province both German and Slovenian are still spoken.

The city of Klagenfurt has been the capital of Carinthia since 1518. Prior to becoming the capital, the city burned twice and was rebuilt both times. The present city was designed by an Italian architect and reflects the style of neighboring Italy, which is only 60 kilometers (36 miles) away.

STYRIA (STEIERMARK)

Carinthia may boast the highest mountain in Austria, but Styria, its neighbor to the east, is home to the Erzberg, known as the mountain of ore. The ore in this mountain is so pure that it can be cut into blocks and carried away to be melted down. Styria is the leading mining province in Austria, and nine-tenths of all iron ore produced nationally comes from the Erzberg.

In addition to iron ore, Styria also produces other minerals such as magnesite and lignite, but mining is only one industry in Styria; agriculture is also very important. About half of the

A vendor wraps up a bottle of pumpkin seed oil.

province is forested, and another quarter is covered with grassland and vineyards. Apple orchards stretch as far as the eye can see, and fields of pumpkins produce pumpkin seed oil, known as the green gold of Styria.

The medieval city of Graz is the provincial capital. It is the second largest city in Austria as well as one of the oldest, having existed as early as 1189. It is an important seat of Austrian government and a center of education, with almost forty thousand students attending three universities.

BURGENLAND

Clinging to the eastern edge of Austria is the province of Burgenland, a land characterized by tree-covered hills and vineyards. Ruins and graves throughout the region attest to the presence of a variety of cultures since the Stone Age, including Celts, Franks, and Romans. In 1648 the area became a part of Hungary and remained a part of that nation until after World War I, when the mostly German-speaking people of Burgenland voted to become a part of Austria.

Burgenland brought valuable agricultural land to Austria. The region's many vineyards produce grapes used to make some of Austria's finest wines. Vegetables and grains also grow well here and are processed in canneries built near the vegetable farms.

Eisenstadt, the capital of Burgenland, is dominated by the Esterhazy castle built during the fourteenth century. For several centuries the Esterhazy family was part of Austria's wealthy and powerful nobility, a class of Austrian society just below royalty.

ROUND AND ROUND THE MAYPOLE

Across Austria every village welcomes spring with a May Day celebration and a maypole or *maibaum*. The maypole consists of a tall spruce selected from the forest. The lower limbs are removed and only a top knot of foliage, looking like a lofty Christmas tree, is left. The pole is stripped of bark and decorated with wreaths and ribbons. The maypole is set up near the *rathaus* (city hall) and is the focal point of May Day festivities.

In some communities the fun begins on the night between April 30 and May 1, which is called *unruhnacht* (night of unrest). During the night, secret loves are made public and pranksters recognize unpopular members of the community by piling junk in front of their doors.

Over the years, the maypole has become a symbol of friendly rivalry among the young men of neighboring villages. Boys or young men of each village must guard their pole because raiders from other villages will sneak into town late at night and try to steal it. Austrian law regards stealing the decorated pole as a custom and not a criminal act. However, if the villagers have already installed the pole in its official place, usually in front of the city hall, cutting down or stealing a rival village's maypole is considered a penal offense.

A maypole stands as a symbol of friendly rivalry among neighboring Austrian towns.

The family encouraged artistic expression, especially in music. In fact, they had their own orchestra, and in 1761 they invited composer Joseph Haydn to live on the estate and serve as music director. While providing musical entertainment for the Esterhazy family, Haydn wrote hundreds of compositions including operas, operettas, symphonies, and sonatas. Haydn's home on the Esterhazy estate has been turned into a museum honoring him and another Burgenland composer, Franz Liszt.

Music lovers are not the only ones drawn to this area, however; many also come for water sports and bird watching. They are drawn primarily to Neusiedler See, Austria's largest lake. This unusual lake is no more than seven feet at its deepest point, and the water is slightly salty because there is no natural outlet to flush the native salts and minerals out of the water. The shallow lake warms quickly in the summer and is a popular recreation area for boaters and swimmers. The lake's ring of wetland marsh also provides an ideal habitat for hundreds of varieties of birds, an attraction for naturalists and bird watchers.

VIENNA (WIEN)

Vienna is both a city and the smallest province in Austria. Its location on the east-west trade route along the Danube has played a major role in its development as a commercially important European city. Its history dates back to the Stone Age and has always centered around the river and its surrounding valley. The land there is rich and fertile and has tempted many travelers to linger—sometimes for centuries, until ousted by the next wave of invaders. During the sixth century B.C., the Celts built a salt-trading town here called Vindomina (White Place). In the first century A.D., the Romans took over and changed the name to Vindobona. They set up their own trade routes and built elaborate defenses. Vindobona eventually became Wien, or Vienna, as it is called in English.

The Romans built walls that enclosed about half of the present city; in the 1100s new walls were added to enlarge the city. Emperor Franz Joseph replaced the old fortifications with the Ringstrasse, a broad boulevard which still circles the inner city on three sides with the Danube completing the circle.

Today the small inner city is filled with elegant hotels and shops and some of the most impressive architecture in Europe. For centuries architects have freely expressed their creativity on the landscape of Vienna, and the city is adorned with stunning

St. Stephen's Cathedral blends several architectural styles and features Vienna's coat of arms on its tiled rooftop.

examples of a wide range of architectural styles. In some cases a single building such as Saint Stephen's Cathedral blends several styles. One of the most interesting features of the cathedral is the colorful tiled roof that displays Vienna's coat of arms. Other striking examples of architecture include the Schloss Schonbrunn, a two-thousand room palace, and Belvedere Palace, built for Prince Eugene of Savoy between 1714 and 1723.

Not only is Vienna known for splendid architecture, it also has an international reputation as a center of the arts, especially music. For centuries Vienna was the capital of the Habsburg monarchy, a supporter of the growth of music and culture in the city. Furthermore, for the Viennese, leading the good life is almost an art form in itself. They take pride in their sophisticated city, its musical heritage, and cultural opportunities. Fine dining, sipping coffee in a coffeehouse or wine in a *Heuriger* (wine tavern) are as much a part of the cultural ambience of Vienna as the operas, concerts, and museums.

Contrasting its image as a cultural center, Vienna is also one of the leading industrial and commercial locations in Europe.

Many metal products, precision instruments, electrical goods, and motors are produced in the area. Vienna is the financial center of Austria and the seat of the federal government.

PULLING THE PIECES TOGETHER

The earliest peoples of Europe followed the flow of the rivers and mountain passes into the area that is now Austria. Some were just passing through; others made their homes in the area for extended periods of time. Regardless, they all contributed to the ethnic and cultural mosaic still apparent in the land today.

2

BUILDING A DYNASTY

A fat little stone doll made twenty-five thousand years ago tells the story of the earliest inhabitants of the land now called Austria. This ancient statuette, the *Venus of Willendorf*, proves that the area around the Danube River was populated as early as the early Stone Age, when humans first began making stone tools and art objects. The Venus, other artifacts, and the frozen body of a man who died approximately fifty-five hundred years ago lead archaeologists through the murky history of human evolution from the use of stone, copper, and bronze to iron tools.

The Iron Age was ushered in around 700 B.C. by the Celts, invaders from the north who followed the Danube into the area. They brought techniques for tunneling underground and mined iron ore to make tools such as plows. They were also the first to effectively mine the land's vast salt deposits.

After the Celts, the Danube brought a procession of invaders and travelers into the land. Among those who came were the Romans, Teutons, Slavs, Huns, Goths, Franks, Bavarians, Avars, and Magyars. No one group gained firm control until the late 700s, when several of Europe's small Germanic States(groups of people who shared similar languages and cultures) loosely joined together to form the Holy Roman Empire. Charlemagne, king of one group called the Franks, was chosen as the first emperor of the Holy Roman Empire. In the rich lands near present-day Vienna, Charlemagne established a territory called the Ostmark (or Eastern March). After his death in 814, ownership of the land was contested until 976, when Leopold of Babenberg became ruler of the Ostmark and renamed the area Osterreich (Austria).

The Babenbergs ruled for almost three hundred years and were, for the most part, wise and benevolent rulers. They increased their territory, established a trade economy, schools, and a public hospital. Encouraged by increased prosperity, they began the legacy of art and culture that would become one of Austria's trademarks. In 1246 the last of the Babenbergs, Duke Friedrich II died, leaving no heirs. Ottokar, the king of Bohemia, a state that would later become Czechoslovakia, took over Austria for a short time, but the monarchy would soon change hands again.

A DYNASTY IS BORN

In 1273 a group of German princes met to choose a new emperor for the Holy Roman Empire. Historian Dorothy Gies McGuigan describes their goals: "the princes were at pains to choose an agreeable and a mediocre man, one on whose neck they might keep a collective foot. Above all they wanted a ruler who would not make the most precious of all crowns [the crown of the Holy Roman emperor] hereditary."[4]

A little-known provincial nobleman, Rudolf of Habsburg, had shown few signs of strong leadership and seemed just the man for their purposes. He was named the new Holy Roman emperor. Rudolf was so surprised by the appointment that he at first thought the messenger was joking. However, one man knew Rudolf's character well enough to suspect that the joke might end up being on the princes. The bishop of Basel, with whom Rudolf had recently been at war, said: "Now sit tight, Lord God, or Rudolf will have Thy throne."[5]

As the bishop predicted, the princes had sadly underestimated Rudolf. A shrewd politician and negotiator, he set about building a dynasty. One of his first acts was to oust Ottokar from Austria and turn over the Austrian duchies (regions ruled by dukes) to his own sons. The Habsburg dynasty ultimately became one of the most powerful

Charlemagne, the first emperor of the Holy Roman Empire, established a territory called Ostmark in the ninth century, near present-day Vienna.

Rudolf of Habsburg does battle with Ottokar II.

and enduring in Europe. It would last for more than six hundred years—well into the twentieth century.

WAGE MATRIMONY NOT WAR

In Rudolf's day and long afterward, the various states of Europe often met on the battlefield to settle their differences or seize new territory. The Habsburgs, however, preferred a more civilized and subtle means of increasing their influence and power. They married their royal sons and daughters to the royal offspring of other powerful states. Alliances formed by royal marriages were not new to Europe, but the Habsburgs carried the practice to new extremes with more frequent and advantageous marriages. Through strategic marriage they gained new wealth, political influence in other countries, and allies for the times when war became necessary. Sometimes the Habsburg bride or groom, or children of the union, eventually gained the throne of their new homeland. The practice of Habsburg royal marriages began as early as Rudolf's reign as Holy Roman emperor, when he betrothed two of his children to two children of King Ottokar.

One of the most crucial Habsburg marriages occurred in 1477. The ruling Habsburg monarch, Emperor Friedrich III, sent his eighteen-year-old son, Maximilian, to marry Maria, daughter and heiress of wealthy and powerful Duke Charles the Bold of Burgundy, a country in the area that is now southern France. Many arranged marriages were loveless unions of convenience, but Maximilian and Maria quickly fell deeply in love. They had two children before Maria died from a fall from a horse. Maximilian remarried, but he never recovered from the loss of his first wife, and he requested that after his death his heart be taken back to Burgundy and placed in the tomb with his beloved Maria. The marriage of Maximilian and Maria was a beautiful and sad love story, but it was also a political event that changed history by enabling the Habsburgs to become a major European power.

THE HOLY ROMAN EMPIRE

The Holy Roman Empire was a loose federation of small European states. The empire existed from 962 to 1806, but its strength varied according to the power of the current emperor and the strength of the church.

In theory the Holy Roman Empire was a civil counterpart to the Catholic Church and stood for the unity of all Christians. It was also meant to be a political organization with one leader over all existing states. It never really fulfilled either premise. The church saw the empire as a secular extension of itself, dedicated to protecting the church and spreading the Christian faith. The emperors, on the other hand, often saw it as the path to their own wealth and power. These different viewpoints caused frequent conflict between the pope and the emperor throughout the existence of the empire.

Gordon Brook-Shepherd, who has written extensively on Austrian history says:

> The process by which the Habsburgs promoted themselves during the space of less than fifty years from a secondary European royal house into a world-wide power without drawing a sword in battle is a dizzy one. . . . At the Duke's [Maria's father, Charles of Burgundy] death in 1478, all the Burgundian possessions, which included the Netherlands, passed into Habsburg hands. Maximilian's only son married in 1496 Princess Joanna of Spain, and their son Charles rounded off the link by marrying the other Iberian [the peninsula comprising Spain and Portugal] heiress, Isabella of Portugal.[6]

The line of heirs begun by Maximilian and Maria culminated in Charles V, who eventually ruled over an empire that stretched from the Danube basin across western Europe and even across the Atlantic to new Spanish possessions in South America. His empire was far too huge for one person to rule effectively, so he divided his territory, giving his Austrian lands to his younger brother, Ferdinand. Ferdinand had been married as an infant to Anne, daughter of King Wladislaw of Poland, and through this union added both Bohemia and Hungary to his holdings, an event that strengthened the Habsburgs' power in Austria and neighboring lands.

Throughout their reign, the Habsburgs continued to strengthen their position through well-planned marriages . In fact, they became so well known for their matrimonial conquests that it was often said, "Let others wage war; you, happy Austria, marry."[7]

FACING CONFLICT

Not even the Habsburgs could solve all of their problems with wedding bells, however, and Ferdinand's Austria faced threats from several fronts. The Turks, led by Süleyman the Magnificent, overran the Balkans and in 1529 laid siege to Vienna. When winter came, the Turks withdrew, but because of their desire for Vienna and the surrounding territory, they continued to be a looming menace. To better protect his interests, Ferdinand moved his court to Vienna in 1533 and became the first of the Habsburgs to reside full-time in the city. This move gave new prestige to the city but did not end the conflict with the Turkish army.

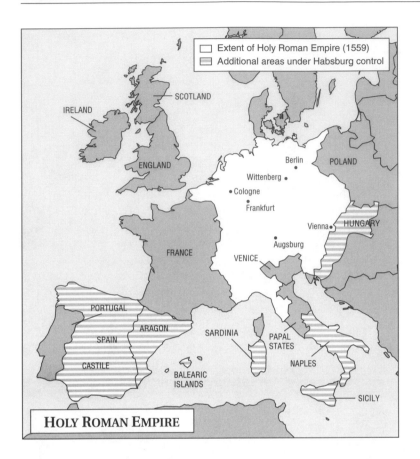

Extent of Holy Roman Empire (1559)
Additional areas under Habsburg control

SCOTLAND
IRELAND
ENGLAND
Berlin
POLAND
Wittenberg
Cologne
Frankfurt
Vienna HUNGARY
Augsburg
FRANCE
VENICE
PORTUGAL
ARAGON
SARDINIA
PAPAL STATES
SPAIN
NAPLES
CASTILE
BALEARIC ISLANDS
SICILY

HOLY ROMAN EMPIRE

It was not until 1683 that the Turks finally left Austria for good. That year, they again laid siege to Vienna. This time Vienna, already weakened by an epidemic of bubonic plague, nearly fell. Christianity was a unifying force in central Europe at the time, however, and the Viennese called on other Christian armies of the area to help push the Moslem Turks to the southeastern edge of Europe.

THE REFORMATION: RELIGIOUS CONFLICT

Even though the Christian forces of western Europe united to drive out the Turks, conflict within their own religion was simmering. Martin Luther, a German peasant turned monk and preacher, attacked the Catholic Church for its rampant corruption. In 1520 after being excommunicated, or excluded, from the Catholic Church, he founded the Protestant movement. One historian writes: "That defiance which placed him in open competition with the Vatican for the souls of men, not only destroyed

Martin Luther criticized the Catholic Church and founded the Prostestant movement.

for ever the unity of Christian faith; it also extinguished any spiritual meaning that was left in the Holy Roman Empire of the Habsburgs."[8]

People living in Habsburg-dominated lands welcomed the doctrines of this movement called the Protestant Reformation, and by the middle of the sixteenth century most of the inhabitants were Protestant. However, the Habsburgs themselves continued to support the Roman Catholic Church. As the result of this support, Catholics in Austria managed to maintain a strong presence. Eventually the German princes split along religious lines into two opposing religious camps, the Evangelical (Protestant) Union and the Catholic League.

In 1619 Ferdinand II of the Austrian Habsburgs, a Catholic, ascended to the throne as Holy Roman emperor. Brook-Shepherd writes that Ferdinand: "was dedicated to wiping out the stain of Protestantism from the earth. Before ascending to the throne, . . . [Ferdinand] had served notice of his religious mission by launching all-out war against the Protestants in his hereditary Austrian lands."[9]

Ferdinand's army destroyed hundreds of Protestant churches and burned Protestant books by the tens of thousands. He tried to extend his offensive throughout the non-Germanic lands in his domain, and in the process he touched off a religious war that would come to be known as the Thirty Years' War. Most of Europe became involved in the long war, which finally ended

TRAVELING FIRST CLASS

In a day when there were no motorized vehicles and few roads, travel of only a few miles could be filled with inconvenience and danger. Yet epic journeys across Europe were common. The European aristocracies established close ties with each other and often traveled great distances for occasions ranging from marriages to tournaments to wars. They traveled as they lived, with great fanfare and ceremony attended by dozens, sometimes hundreds, of aides and servants. In his book *The Habsburgs: Portrait of a Dynasty*, Edward Crankshaw describes life on the road during the Middle Ages:

During all this time medieval Europe was being hammered out into more or less the final form which was to endure until the twentieth century. It was an age of perpetual movement. Emperors, kings, princes, prince bishops, knights and men-at-arms made incessant and incredible journeys, brilliantly appareled [dressed] on their heavy horses, joining in constantly changing alliances, combining the business of their imperial, royal, or princely masters with their pursuit of private gain, pausing to draw up a battle-line and putting on their heavy armour to confront the enemy of the moment, meeting each other in elaborate tournaments when there was no battle to be fought, journeying over roads, over snowy mountain passes from one end of Europe to the other to make an advantageous marriage, unfolding their silken tents, streaming their pennants and banners, setting out their gold and silver plate all carried in their baggage trains like so many travelling circuses. While the princes, as a rule, kept their dignity, their loutish [rude or ill-mannered] followers kept up a tumult of brawling and noisy quarreling, duelling and murder.

in 1648 with the signing of the Peace of Westphalia. This document gave rulers the right to settle the religious question in their respective territories.

RECONSTRUCTION AND NEW PROBLEMS

Reconstruction of Austria's social, political, and economic systems destroyed by the war began under Ferdinand III, who ruled from 1637 until his death in 1657. His son, Leopold I, who held the throne from his father's death through 1705, continued the reconstruction. Ferdinand and Leopold struggled to reestablish Catholicism as Austria's dominant religion while fighting continued Turkish invasions along their eastern borders. Due to reconstruction and war, they were faced with financial problems as well; however, they found time and resources to continue the Habsburg tradition of patronizing the arts.

Leopold in particular set out to rebuild Vienna after the Turkish siege of 1683 and encouraged Austria's finest archi-

After the Thirty Years' War, Austria's reconstruction period continued under Leopold I.

tects to design new buildings in the most popular architectural styles of the day. Fine arts and music also flourished in the atmosphere of artistic revival. But the huge Habsburg dynasty was beginning to break apart.

King Charles II of Spain, a Habsburg, died in 1700, and both Austria and France had ties to and claimed the Spanish throne. Another war, the War of Spanish Succession, broke out and split the mighty Habsburg empire in two. Austria gained Belgium and Spanish land in Italy, but France won the Spanish crown.

The unity of the remaining Austrian Habsburg empire was put in jeopardy when Leopold's second son, Charles VI, ascended to the throne. He had no sons to follow him, and the Habsburgs had never had a female ruler. To keep the dynasty intact, Charles pushed through an agreement that made his daughter, Maria Theresa, his successor.

MARIA THERESA'S REIGN

Maria Theresa was twenty-three years old when she took the Habsburg throne in 1740. The Austria she controlled, though still powerful, was a nation close to ruin. Historian Edward Crankshaw describes the new queen's ascension to the throne:

> The young queen had no money, no army, virtually no central administration; worse still, no sensible advisers. At twenty-three, untrained, armed only with her beauty, her youth, her trust in God, and a character the strength of which neither she nor anybody else could yet appreciate, she stood at the head of a bankrupt empire, or collection of lands, which her father had brought to the edge of ruin. When she was acquainted by one of her elderly ministers with the true state of the realm she behaved with perfect calm and self-possession; but afterwards, alone with her favourite lady-in-waiting, she burst into tears.[10]

The new queen was immediately besieged by neighbors who had been waiting for a moment of weakness to seize Habsburg territory. The ensuing war, known as the War of Austrian Succession (1740–1748), tested Maria Theresa's mettle as a leader. The war ended favorably for Austria. However, Prussia, which took Silesia early in the conflict, still held it after the war.

*Maria Theresa ascended
the Austrian throne in
1740.*

Initially Maria Theresa ruled with the wiles of a girl. She used cajolery and pleading to win support and get things done. But she quickly gained wisdom and maturity and learned the art of commanding. She also rid herself of her father's incompetent staff and began to surround herself with excellent advisers.

According to historian Crankshaw, the first adviser she added to her staff would become almost a father figure to her. Don Manuel Telles de Menezes e Castro was a shrewd and talented diplomat. The queen offered him the position of adviser with these instructions: "to show me my faults and make me recognize them. . . . This being most necessary for a ruler, since there are few or none at all to be found who will do this, commonly refraining out of awe or self-interest."[11] He accepted the challenge and remained her close confidant and adviser until his death thirty years later.

Maria Theresa was not always the victor in war. Barely eight years after the War of Austrian Succession, she joined an alliance with France and Russia against Prussia and Britain. Prussia and Britain won this war, known as the Seven Years' War, and Maria Theresa did not fulfill her hope of regaining Silesia.

For the most part, Maria Theresa's forty-year reign was an era of prosperity and development for Austria. She started a public education system as well as a civil service, and reformed the army. She also managed to get her husband, whom she married in 1736, elected as emperor of the Holy Roman Empire, a title held by a Habsburg almost continuously since Rudolf I. The empress, who enjoyed the arts, and especially music, helped build Vienna's reputation as a music center. Maria Theresa continued the Habsburg tradition of politically motivated marriages, when she married off her youngest daughter, Marie Antoinette, to Louis XVI of France.

After Maria Theresa's death in 1780, two of her sons ruled briefly before following her in death. In 1792 her grandson became head of the Habsburg monarchy and was named Holy Roman Emperor Francis II.

THE NAPOLEONIC WARS

The French Revolution, which began in 1789, brought an end to the French-Austrian alliance built on Marie Antoinette's marriage; in 1792 revolutionary France declared war on Austria. When the revolution ended in 1799, Napoleon Bonaparte became dictator and eventually emperor of France, ultimately conquering much of Europe.

In Austria Francis II suffered major defeats at the hands of Napoleon. Because of the French domination of Germany, Francis feared that Napoleon could become the next Holy Roman emperor. To prevent this from happening, he declared himself Francis I, Emperor of Austria, renounced the title of Holy Roman emperor, and dissolved the Holy Roman Empire. The end of the Holy Roman Empire did not end the hostilities between France and Austria, however; in 1809 Austria was again defeated by Napoleon's greater military strength.

After this defeat, Francis appointed Klemens von Metternich, a nobleman and political leader, as foreign minister. Metternich (who ultimately became Austria's chancellor) brought reconciliation with France by arranging a marriage between Francis's daughter, Marie Louise, and Napoleon. But the alliance was short lived. In 1813 Austria took advantage of Napoleon's failing position and once again declared war on France in order to regain lost territory. Although Austria was victorious, the war took its toll on financial and human resources, seriously weakening the country.

When the war ended, treaty negotiations took place at the Congress of Vienna. European allies met from September 1814

As Austria's foreign minister, Klemens von Metternich (pictured) attempted to reconcile Austria's tenuous relationship with France by arranging a marriage between Marie Louise and Napoleon.

to June 1815 to draw up the terms of the Second Treaty of Paris. Here Metternich, the guiding force of the congress, served his emperor well. The Austrian empire accepted the loss of Belgium and parts of Galicia, but regained Lombardy, Salzburg, and the Tyrol, and expanded to include Venetia, Istria, and Dalmatia, states located along the Adriatic Sea. The Holy Roman Empire was not reinstated, but a new confederation of all of the German states was put into place, with Austria in control.

After his triumph at the Congress of Vienna, Metternich continued to work to make the Habsburg empire the center of the new European order. But, on the home front, little was being done to improve conditions for the peasants. Poor wages, inadequate housing, and lack of civil rights bred discontent. The resulting rebel revolt in 1848 forced Metternich to resign and go into exile and Emperor Ferdinand (who became emperor following Francis's death in 1835) to abdicate the throne. Ferdinand's young nephew Franz Joseph was next in line to lead the monarchy.

THE LAST EMPEROR

"Farewell, my youth"[12] murmured the eighteen-year-old Franz Joseph as he donned the crown of the Habsburgs in 1848. At eighteen he was at the head of an empire of forty million people, an empire embroiled in domestic strife. He would reign as emperor of Austria for sixty-eight years, longer than any other head of state except Louis XIV of France. It would be a reign fraught with conflict and personal heartbreak for the emperor. Yet it would also be a time of economic prosperity and continued artistic excellence for Austria.

In the beginning the new emperor was faced with three difficult issues. He needed to establish his political authority in the empire, end a rebellion that had begun in Hungary and assure Habsburg authority there, and reassert Austrian leadership of the German Confederation, the alliance of German states. He first dealt with the revolt of his own people. After enduring years of poor economic conditions and no civil rights, they wanted a constitution and some voice in their own affairs. He gave them a constitution that guaranteed individual liberties and equality and established a centralized government; just two years later, however, he revoked the constitution.

With some of the problems at home taken care of, Franz Joseph turned his attention to maintaining Austria's position as leader of the German Confederation. But Otto von Bismarck, the new prime minister of Prussia, wanted to unify Germany and make Prussia its leader. This conflict brought about a seven-week war in 1866, which ended in defeat for Austria.

Franz Joseph had hoped that strong support from Hungary would improve his chances in the war. To gain that support and at the same time end his conflict with the Hungarians, he promised to make Hungary equal to Austria. Although Franz Joseph lost the war even with Hungarian support, he honored his promise: The dual Austro-Hungarian monarchy was created in 1867 with Franz Joseph as emperor of Austria and king of Hungary. The two countries would be equal under one ruler. They would share defense, economic and foreign policies, but each would have its own government and constitution.

FRANZ JOSEPH AND SISI

With his three major issues behind him, Franz Joseph could concentrate on ruling a large multiethnic empire. For the most part, it was a time of progress and prosperity for Austria. Yet the emperor was also faced with a long series of personal losses.

One of his early goals as emperor was to find a suitable wife who would bear him children and continue the royal line. On first sight, he fell deeply in love with his beautiful, vivacious young cousin, Elisabeth of Bavaria—affectionately known as Sisi. Brook-Shepherd describes the country's reaction to the announcement in 1853 of the royal engagement:

> First the little town of Bad Ischl, then the Salzkammergut and then the whole empire around exploded with delight. From end to end of the Monarchy, church bells rang, bonfires were lit on mountain peaks, soldiers cheered and waved their caps on parade grounds and priests went down on their knees to pray for divine blessing and a plentiful progeny.[13]

Their marriage began like a fairy tale romance, but after giving birth to a son and two daughters, Sisi became self-absorbed and restless. Even though Franz Joseph's devotion to her never wavered, they seldom saw each other; she spent most of her life traveling the world in an almost frantic need to always be somewhere else. Because she was never around, Sisi even

helped arrange a mistress for Franz Joseph. It was a relationship that the emperor would cherish for many years although
his true love continued to be his elusive wife.

The End of the Habsburg Dynasty

Sisi was assassinated by an Italian anarchist in 1898. Her death
was the third in a series of family tragedies deeply affecting the
emperor. Almost ten years earlier, their thirty-one-year-old
son shot and killed his seventeen-year-old mistress, then put
the gun to his own head to join her in death. And the emperor's
brother, Maximilian, emperor of Mexico, had been executed
by rebels in 1867.

*In 1867, Franz Joseph
became emperor of the
Austro-Hungarian
monarchy.*

With Franz Joseph's only son gone, his grandnephew, Franz
Ferdinand, was next in line to inherit the throne. The aging emperor, however, despised the young man. His feelings toward
his nephew worsened when Franz Ferdinand defied him and
the monarchy by marrying Countess Sophia Chotek, who was
not of royal blood. In the eyes of the emperor and his court,
Countess Sophia was not good enough to be a Habsburg bride.

By 1914 Franz Joseph saw Russian-backed Serbia as the
principal threat to the security of Austria-Hungary because
Serbia supported anti-Habsburg groups and activities in the
states of Bosnia and Herzegovina. Ignoring the counsel of his
advisers, Franz Ferdinand insisted on a state visit to Sarajevo,
Bosnia. He had been invited to review the Bosnian military
and saw it as a chance to build his image as the future emperor. As Franz Ferdinand and his wife Sophia rode through
the city on June 28, 1914, they were assassinated by Bosnian
rebels. Assuming Serbian involvement, Emperor Franz
Joseph declared war on Serbia a month later on July 28. The
war escalated into World War I and brought about the end of
the 642-year-old Habsburg dynasty.

3

BUILDING A MODERN NATION

The conflict that began with the brutal double murder in Sarajevo rapidly spread across Europe and became the First World War. New technology made it a war of such intensity and violence that people fervently declared it to be "the war to end all wars." The editors of *Austria: A Country Study* report the steps through which the regional conflict flared into a global war:

> Russia's decision to mobilize on July 30 escalated the war beyond a regional conflict by bringing into play the system of European alliances [agreements between nations to protect one another]. . . . Thus, Germany responded to Russia's mobilization by immediately declaring war on France and Russia. On August 4, Britain declared war on Germany. On August 6, Austria-Hungary declared war on Russia. Finally, on August 12, France and Britain declared war on Austria-Hungary.[14]

The weakening Austro-Hungarian empire lost more ground when Emperor Franz Joseph died on November 21, 1916, leaving Austria with no strong leader. The heir apparent, Franz Joseph's grandnephew Karl I, was a young man little suited to wearing the mantle of imperial leadership. Dorothy Gies McGuigan writes:

> Had [Karl] been born in another age, in a time of peace and an era of kings, he would have been a very nice emperor indeed: gentle, kind, earnest, almost pathetically eager to do the right thing. A touch of the scholar, a touch of the saint: too frail, however, for the insufferable burden that now fell to him.[15]

By the time the new emperor came to power, however, even if he had been a stronger leader, he could do little to change the course of the war. The fate of the Habsburg monarchy depended not on the actions of the emperor, but on the outcome of the war.

In April 1917 the United States joined with the Allies—Britain, France, and Russia—bringing fresh troops and equipment into the conflict, an event that experts believe hastened the end of the war. On November 3, 1918, an armistice ended Austria-Hungary's participation in World War I; the Allies had won. On November 11, Karl I stepped down leaving Austria without a monarch for the first time in almost a thousand years.

AN UNSTABLE REPUBLIC

When the war ended, the Allies divided the Austro-Hungarian empire into several nations, one of which is present-day Austria. The peace treaty they drafted stated that Austria could not form any alliances with Germany. This provision kept Austria, now a small impoverished nation, from regaining its former power. The loss of so much land also robbed Austria of many of its natural resources, and the neighboring countries once under its control were not willing to make up the shortages. Suffering from war damage and poverty, many urban areas were soon on the verge of famine. The social atmosphere was ripe for political movements to win converts with promises of a better life.

Politically the Austrian people divided into three opposing camps, and no one of the three held a strong majority. The Social Democratic Party (SDAF) supported the use of democratic meth-

AUSTRO-HUNGARIAN EMPIRE AFTER WWI

GERMANY

USSR

POLAND

CZECHOSLOVAKIA

SWITZERLAND

Vienna •

AUSTRIA

HUNGARY

ROMANIA

SOUTH TYROL

YUGOSLAVIA

ITALY

Sarajevo •

Adriatic Sea

☐ Austro-Hungarian Empire before division

Adolf Hitler studied art in Vienna and went on to rule Germany and Austria during World War II.

ods to establish working-class rule. The Christian Social Party (CSP) was a conservative democratic party based on Christian values. The third major party, the Greater German People's Party—commonly called the Nationals—was anti-Semitic and believed in protecting national interests and social freedoms. A small radical portion of the Nationals formed the National Socialist German Workers' Party (NSDAP), or Nazi Party. This new racist and anti-Semitic party was neither large nor influential during the 1920s. A similar party was founded in Germany and was eventually led by Adolf Hitler.

HITLER AND THE NAZIS

Hitler was a child of Austria. He was born in Braunau in Upper Austria and spent most of his childhood in that province. In 1907 when he was eighteen, he moved to Vienna to study art. His dream of an art career never materialized, but during his six years in Vienna he began to hate the Jews. John Putnam, a writer for *National Geographic* describes the young Hitler as:

a young man from the provinces who wanted to be an artist. He failed as an artist, but learned much that he would later find useful. . . . He absorbed the exhortations [persuasive urgings] of one Georg Ritter von Schonerer, a member of parliament; "Religion's only a disguise, in the blood the foulness lies." Von Schonerer's followers wore on their watch chains the insignia of the anti-Semite, a hanged Jew. "Wherever I went," the young man [Hitler] would write, "I began to see Jews, and the more I saw, the more sharply they became distinguished in my eyes from the rest of humanity. . . . Gradually I began to hate them." After six years, Adolf Hitler left Vienna for Germany.[16]

Once in Germany, the would-be artist honed his hatreds and sharpened his political skills. He developed a charismatic personality that drew disillusioned people to his vision of a better world. In 1926 with Hitler as its leader, the German Nazi Party united with the Austrian Nazis despite some differences in beliefs. It was a unity that would simmer for several years, then prove disastrous for Austria.

ECONOMIC AND SOCIAL DECLINE

Meanwhile, the new Austria was struggling with the problems of establishing an unfamiliar form of government. The CSP was voted into power, and its leader, Ignaz Seipel, was chosen to serve as chancellor (or prime minister). The editors of *Austria: A Country Study* report:

> In 1922 [Ignaz Seipel] assumed the office of chancellor. By adroitly [skillfully] manipulating the European political situation and accepting renewed prohibitions on union with Germany, he managed to obtain foreign loans to launch an economic stabilization plan. Although the plan stabilized the currency and set state finances on a sound course, it provided no solution to the underlying economic problems and dislocation, and it extracted a high social cost by cutting government social programs and raising taxes.[17]

Despite Seipel's efforts, social and economic conditions in Austria continued to worsen. From 1929 until 1933, unemployment more than doubled, rising from 280,000 to nearly 600,000. Hungry and disillusioned people began rethinking their political allegiance. They expressed their discontent both in street violence and at the polls. During this time, Nazism was becoming more and more popular in Austria. In 1932 and again in 1933, the Austrian Nazi Party made significant gains in local elections.

While the Nazis were gaining strength, Austria was under the control of Engelbert Dollfuss, a leader in the CSP. Dollfuss, who wanted to be dictator of Austria, ended the parliamentary government and formed the Fatherland Front. He intended for the front to displace the existing political parties in an effort to make his organization more powerful. Although Dollfuss declared the front the only legal political organization, the other political parties did not disband but went underground.

With German support, the Austrian Nazi Party tried to take over the Dollfuss government in 1934 and force the appointment of a Nazi-dominated government. The coup failed, but Dollfuss was killed. His successor, Chancellor Kurt von Schuschnigg, did not understand the extent of the control that Hitler and the Nazis were gaining in Austria. He tried to keep peace by making agreements with Hitler, but the agreements he signed in 1936 and 1938 only served to tighten the Nazi grip on Austria.

The Nazis' strong influence was not what Schuschnigg wanted for Austria, so despite his agreements with the Germans, he began secretly planning a last attempt to save Austrian

Hitler's Nazis ultimately forced Austrian chancellor Kurt von Schuschnigg (pictured here) to resign.

The Anschluss *(annexation of Austria) reflected the Austrians' widespread desire for change but not necessarily their support for Hitler and the Nazis.*

sovereignty. He decided to take the issue to the people and allow them to vote to preserve Austria as a sovereign nation.

Hitler, who saw a yes vote as a symbolic defeat for Germany and the Nazi Party, bombarded the Austrian chancellor with threats that he would forcefully take over Austria. Under pressure, Schuschnigg agreed to cancel the ballot and tender his resignation. Schuschnigg's actions could not stop Hitler, however, and on March 12, 1938, the German army marched into Austria.

THE *ANSCHLUSS*

The Austrians made little attempt to stop the takeover and the *Anschluss* (annexation) was declared. The annexation made Austria a part of Nazi Germany and Adolf Hitler, its new leader. The *Anschluss* was popular with the people; however, the editors of *Austria: A Country Study* write that: "the positive vote reflected the Austrians' desire for change far more than it did widespread support for Hitler and Nazism."[18]

Hitler's government won even stronger support from the Austrian people by taking steps to solve some of the country's economic problems and relieve social distress. He created new jobs, for example, and revitalized industry. In less than a year, Austria's economy had improved and the unemployment rate was dropping rapidly. These efforts not only won Hitler more popular support but also prepared Austria for contributing to the German war machine.

Not all of the Austrian population reaped the benefits of the new prosperity, however. Nazi rule brought with it political repression and barbaric racial policies. And Austria's Jews were the primary targets. Although Austria had been traditionally anti-Semitic, the Jewish population (numbering around 220,000 in 1938) had full civil rights and was prominent in economic, political, and cultural life, especially in Vienna.

In the weeks following the *Anschluss*, violent anti-Semitic attacks were common. Initially the attacks were individual acts of violence, but soon they became well-organized and legally sanctioned actions. At first the new Nazi government passed laws that took away the civil rights of Jews and eventually forced most of them out of Austria altogether. About 150,000 Jews left Austria before October 1941, when the emigration policy was

FLEEING NAZI AUSTRIA: ONE FAMILY'S STORY

Not all Austrians embraced the annexation with Hitler's Germany. Many feared for their lives when the annexation occurred and secretly fled the country. One example, familiar to most Americans, is the Georg von Trapp family of Salzburg, whose story was told in the popular 1965 film, *The Sound of Music*.

After his wife died, Trapp married Maria Kutschera, a former nun who had come to work as a governess for the Trapp children. When the Austrian national bank failed and the last of the family fortunes disappeared, Maria and the nine children began to earn money by singing in public. As the family was building a musical reputation, Georg von Trapp was speaking out against the Nazis. So when Hitler took over Austria, the Trapps found themselves in trouble with the Nazis. They secretly left home, friends, and belongings, and fled the country. The Trapp family eventually immigrated to the United States, where they continued their musical career.

The Nazis built many concentration camps during World War II, including this one in Linz, Austria.

discontinued. It was replaced by a new policy that called for the extermination of all Jews. The Nazis built twenty-one concentration camps in Austria; Jews and other minorities were imprisoned in the camps and then killed. Approximately 60,000 Austrian Jews died in those camps. Although their loss was by far the greatest, the Jews were not the only people targeted by German racism. About 35,000 Austrian Slavic minorities, including Czechs, Slovaks, Slovenes, and Croats were also deported or killed under Nazi rule.

WORLD WAR II

In September 1939, Germany invaded Poland, and the world was at war again, a war that would take an even higher toll in life and property than World War I. Technically Austria did not participate in World War II because it did not exist as a nation; it was a part of Germany. However, 800,000 Austrians were drafted into the German army, and another 150,000 served in the Waffen SS, an elite Nazi military unit. Most served loyally and willingly, especially during the early years of the war.

As part of Germany, Austria once again found itself fighting against the Allied powers, Great Britain, France, the Soviet Union, and the United States. And once again, the Allies would win the war. By 1943 Allied attacks on Austria had become frequent and destructive, and in the spring of 1945 the Soviet

THE SECRET OF THE LAKE

In 1945 Austrian farmers were called out late at night to help Nazi soldiers lug large wooden crates to the shores of Lake Toplitz in the Salzkammergut. Rumors have been flying ever since about what the crates held, and where they are now. Treasure hunters dream of a submerged cache rich in gold, art treasures, and priceless documents that disappeared in World War II.

Over the years, several expeditions have attempted to discover the lake's secrets. Divers have brought to the surface a lackluster haul of counterfeit pound notes (designed to weaken the British economy), a few false stamps, dynamite, weapons and other war relics, but no fabulous treasure.

The rumors of treasure persist, however, and in June 2000 the producers of CBS's current affairs show *60 Minutes II*, launched another expedition. "We don't know for certain if there's anything down there, but we're interested in finding World War II–era artifacts and historically relevant documents from the secret police," Bill Owens of CBS told reporters.

The lake is 1.2 miles (2 km) long, 1,312 feet (400 meters) wide and 338 feet (103 meters) deep. At a depth of 65 feet, there is no oxygen, and sunlight does not penetrate the murky water. The complete lack of oxygen prevents items from ever rotting or rusting, so anything submerged there should be well preserved.

Oceaneering, the engineering company that helped recover valuables from the *Titanic*, is providing the technical expertise for the CBS team. A remotely operated vehicle will sketch the exact landscape of the lake bottom. "This is the first comprehensive look at the lake. Areas not covered before

 will be covered once and for all," said Owens, who hopes, along with many others, that Lake Toplitz will finally give up its secrets.

Divers retrieve forged money from Lake Toplitz.

Union's Red Army entered Austrian territory and captured Vienna.

The war left Austria crippled by loss. Industrial and agricultural capabilities as well as homes and businesses were destroyed. Cathedrals and historical buildings were piles of rubble. And many people died in the conflict; 250,000 people were killed in action, and another 25,000 civilians died as a result of bombing or military actions.

A DEFEATED PEOPLE

After Germany's surrender, the Allies reestablished Austria as an independent nation and held it responsible for its participation in the war. They divided the country into four zones to be controlled by the four Allied powers. Vienna was divided separately into a zone for each of the Allies, and each of the four powers controlled the city center on a rotating monthly basis. The situation added to the confusion of a defeated nation struggling to establish a stable government and a sense of national identity.

The new postwar Austrian government was established under the supervision of the Allies. This new government, known as the Second Republic, faced a desperate situation. The German surrender to the Allies ended the fighting but brought no relief to the Austrians. Although a new government had been established, Austria was still under the control of the four Allied powers. Each of those countries maintained large occupational forces in the country to ensure that all terms of the treaty were followed. The cost of this Allied occupation had to be borne by Austria and took as much as 35 percent of the national budget. In addition, about 3 million noncitizens including foreign soldiers, refugees, and displaced persons were in the country. They all needed food, housing, and medical care.

The economy was in chaos. Railroads and communication lines were out of operation and about 177,000 homes were partly or completely destroyed. The Soviets seized industrial equipment in their zone. Agricultural output was approximately half of prewar levels, and the total value of the nation's output of goods and services was about one-third of the pre–World War I level. Fueled by desperate shortages, the black market dominated the flow of goods. In a speech at Christmastime in 1945, Chancellor Leopold Figl expressed the hopelessness of the situation with these words: "I can give you

A crumbling postwar Vienna was divided into zones by each of the four allied powers.

nothing, not even candles for your Christmas tree. I can only ask you to have faith in Austria."[19]

AUSTRIA REBUILDS

The people's faith in Austria, bolstered by strong leadership and outside sources of economic aid, eventually began paying off. The new government took control of many industries that were important to rebuilding: mining, chemical plants, steel construction, and mechanical engineering. It also stabilized the currency and negotiated price and wage agreements. Through the Marshall Plan, a program for providing aid to European countries after the war, the United States provided the funds needed for rebuilding. Between 1945 and 1952, Austria received $1.4 billion in aid from the United States. One historian described the remarkable recovery and sustained economic expansion that followed as an economic miracle.

With restored prosperity, Austria's attention turned to ending the four-power occupation. However, negotiations were slow.

Russia and the Western Allies were squabbling, and issues else-where were drawing attention away from Austria. Finally in 1955, the four Allied powers signed the Austrian State Treaty, ending the military occupation and preventing the permanent division of Austria. It also forbade unification with Germany and the restoration of Habsburg rule.

BUILDING A MODERN NATION

During the occupation, and in the years that followed, the Austrians set out to rebuild their cities and regain the cultural sophistication that they, especially the Viennese, had long enjoyed. As the image of a nation of artistic and cultural excellence was revitalized, it was matched with a new image of Austria as a modern industrialized nation. Gradually, the employment structure changed from primarily agriculture and mining to industry. By 1959, 41 percent of the work force worked in industry. This shift helped bring Austrian income levels up to a par with those of neighboring countries.

Chancellor Bruno Kreisky brought renewed prosperity to modern Austria.

Although Austria's economy has suffered slumps over the years, overall it has maintained a healthy level of growth and prosperity. In the years between his appointment in 1970 and his resignation in 1983, Chancellor Bruno Kreisky brought about much of this renewed prosperity. For example, when economic growth came to a sudden end after the 1973 oil crisis, Kreisky responded with a plan based on accomplishing two main goals: high employment and low inflation. Kreisky's popularity as well as his political and economic skills enabled him to achieve these goals. Sigurd Pacher states that: "In 1975, unemployment in Austria was 2.0 percent compared with 4.7 percent in West Germany and 8.5 percent in the United States. Besides, inflation never reached two-digit numbers."[20]

In addition to enhancing economic prosperity, Kreisky also tackled a number of social issues. For example, he cut the workweek to forty hours and improved employee benefits. Under his influence, the parliament also passed new legislation that provided for the equality of women. Kreisky passed the Equal Treatment Law in 1979 which demanded equal pay for equal work regardless of gender.

In spite of Kreisky's accomplishments, several issues divided the country and began to undermine his popularity. The most divisive issues included abortion, nuclear power, and ethnic minority rights. A new law passed in 1973 legalized abortion during the first trimester, but opposition backed by the Catholic Church challenged the law. In the spring of 1976, parliament upheld the law. In response to the international energy crisis of the early seventies Kreisky began construction of a nuclear power plant. However, due to public concern, the plant never opened. The Kreisky administration addressed the third issue, ethnic rights, by putting up dual-language signs in communities, such as Burgenland and Carinthia, that have more than a 20 percent ethnic population, people who do not speak German. This brought about violent confrontations, and the German-speaking population ripped the signs down.

All in all, the Kreisky years were good ones, and Austria enjoyed unprecedented prosperity. But by 1983 Kreisky's party had lost some of its popular support, and Kreisky resigned rather than head a government in which his party would lead jointly with another party.

In the years since Kreisky, Austria has returned to the private sector many of the industries that were nationalized after World War II. And although the country still enjoys an affluent economy, unemployment rates and the federal deficit have risen. The higher unemployment rates have brought about resentment of the influx of foreign workers. On the plus side, Austria has become a member of the European Union; tax reforms have reduced the tax burden for business and industry; and the Austrian schilling has become one of the most stable currencies in the world.

4

INFRASTRUCTURE: MAKING THE MACHINERY HUM

Austria's evolution from small, little-known duchy to far-reaching powerful empire to poverty-stricken republic to modern nation has been a fascinating saga. Austria today is a small but solid nation with a healthy market economy and a high standard of living.

A FLEDGLING DEMOCRACY

Change was the key word for Austria's government from the end of Habsburg rule until the 1950s. And the new republic formed after World War II faced some difficult years. Between 1914 and 1950, for example, Austria had five different forms of government and four different currencies. Still, for a nation with little experience in democracy, Austria achieved remarkable success in building a stable new democratic government, a success the country has maintained for more than fifty years.

The head of state in the Austrian government is the president, who is elected for a six-year term. The president, in turn, appoints a chancellor who heads the federal government and is the nation's most influential political figure. Even so, the chancellor governs only with the approval of the parliament, which consists of two houses—the National Council (*Nationalrat*) whose members are elected by the people every four years and the Federal Council (*Bundesrat*) whose members are elected by the provincial legislatures. Additionally, each of the nine federal provinces has its own provincial governor and legislative assembly. Each province controls local issues and sends representatives to the Federal Council.

Austria also has a strong political party system, yet the most powerful parties have traditionally worked together effectively in coalition or joint governments. The Social Democrats, for ex-

rmed a ruling coalition with the Austrian People's
P) in the 1990 election. That coalition remained in
ten years but gradually lost legislative seats as a third
Freedom Party, gained public support. By 1999, the
Party posed a serious threat to the existing coalition.

S FROM THE PAST

ruary 1, 2000, the Freedom Party and the OVP an-
d they were joining to form a new governing coalition.
reement meant that for the first time, the foreigner-
Freedom Party would participate in the ruling coalition.
world was shocked and concerned that a party with such
e political views was leading a national government. In
response, Austria's fourteen European Union (EU) partners
levied political sanctions against Austria and condemned the
extremist new government. The situation also reminded the EU
members why they had formed their partnership in the first
place. The French president of the EU's parliament, Nicole
Fontaine said, "A unifying electric shock has reminded Europeans what unites them the most and what some seem to have
forgotten—peace, liberty and democracy."[21]

The Hofburg palace in Vienna houses the offices of the president.

A UNIFIED EUROPE

The EU grew out of a vision of a unified Europe. It is an organization of European states devoted to establishing consistent policies on matters concerning all European countries. The union seeks to simplify business transactions among member nations and to build Europe's place in world markets by integrating the economies of Western Europe and introducing a common currency, the euro. The EU also tries to ease transactions between member nations and smooth the transition for people moving from one EU country to another.

The EU members join forces in matters such as security, foreign policy, economic controls, human rights, and environmental protection. The presidency of the union rotates every six months among the member countries. Branches of the EU are located in several European cities; for instance, the parliament is headquartered in Strasbourg (France), the council in Brussels (Belgium), and the court of justice in Luxembourg. The country currently serving as president hosts general meetings.

The fifteen full members of the EU are Austria, Belgium, Britain, Denmark, Finland, France, Germany, Greece, Ireland, Italy, Luxembourg, the Netherlands, Portugal, Spain, and Sweden. Discussions are currently under way regarding accepting new members from central and Eastern Europe.

Much of the world's negative reaction was directed toward the party leader, Joerg Haider, who was best known for remarks appearing to play down Nazi crimes during World War II. Haider's soft view of Nazi atrocities during the war and his party's strong stance against foreign workers ignited a firestorm in European politics. European countries, whether former supporters of Hitler's Third Reich or its victims, have spent more than fifty years overcoming the bloody stain of Nazism. They took Haider's right-wing views as a slap in the face.

Nevertheless, the Freedom Party rapidly built strength in Austria because the charismatic Haider painted an attractive political picture for his supporters. His platform is based on protecting Austria's national interests by controlling immigration and unchecked global markets. He promises to end job loss to immigrants and to provide job security and social benefits. He claims that he will eliminate corruption and curtail abuses of the welfare state.

However, Haider's opponents see him as a dangerous right-wing extremist and accuse him of exploiting Austria's growing disenchantment with its current ruling parties. Furthermore, they worry because he has made anti foreigner and racist statements throughout his political career. His 1999 campaign posters, for example, showed Haider and his candidate for prime minister as "Two real Austrians,"[22] a slogan that implies that immigrants are not real Austrians.

Haider's well-known statements seeming to applaud Nazism are also troublesome for many people. In 1991, for example, as governor of Carinthia, he praised the Third Reich for creating new jobs, but did not mention that most of those jobs involved military buildup, slave labor, and concentration camps. He also described Walter Reder, an Austrian major in the Nazi SS who was ultimately convicted of mass murder, as "a soldier who had done his duty."[23]

Faced with the unyielding reaction of other European nations, Haider stepped down from his position as head of the Freedom Party on May 1, 2000. Despite his resignation, the Freedom Party retained its position in the government, and Haider is still very influential in the party, a fact that continues to concern the EU.

Joerg Haider, leader of Austria's Freedom Party, has drawn criticism for downplaying Nazi crimes during World War II.

"A PRO-EUROPEAN COUNTRY"

By mid-June the Austrian response to the EU sanctions was heating up. Many Austrians claim that the sanctions are unjustified and an overreaction. In a statement made in London on June 9, 2000, Austrian foreign minister Benita Ferrero-Waldner said:

> Suddenly people think that we are a half-Nazi country, . . .
> this is terrible because the reality is exactly the contrary.
> Austria has been doing a lot to counter its past and is today a very open, tolerant and pro-European country. . . .
> But . . . the public opinion [of the Austrian people who are]
> already very much frustrated is getting hotter and hotter
> to such a point that maybe then we will not be able to find
> a compromise that is supported by our population.[24]

Many Austrians feel unfairly treated because they believe that other European countries are experiencing similar politics. Stefan Tissot, a young businessman from Upper Austria, for example, says, "Why single out Austria? Neo-Nazism is rampant across Europe."[25] And David Boratav of the London-based European Council on Refugees and Exiles agrees that the problem is widespread, "We face a trend of increased racism and xenophobia [fear and hatred of foreigners] in Europe and can't single out one country. Legislation in the UK [United Kingdom] and Austria is comparable."[26]

These people do have a point. Jean-Marie Le Pen, leader of France's Front National Party, for instance, claims that the races are not equal and is known for his anti-Semitic attitude and references to the Nazi death camps as just a minor detail of World War II. And in Germany, Harly Karg, chairperson of a forum involved in monitoring racism and neo-Nazism, has collected many neo-Nazi leaflets, some of which she says have been handed out in schools.

Yet these examples do not lessen the reaction to Austria's right-wing politics, perhaps because of the country's dark history. Adolf Hitler was, after all, a native Austrian, and some in Europe feel that Austria was all too quick to welcome him and rally around him in the days before World War II.

Despite continued concern, in late June 2000 the EU partners made the first move toward lifting the sanctions on Austria when it agreed to abide by the advice of a panel of three experts chosen specifically to assess Austria's commitment to human rights and to examine the evolution of the Freedom

AUSTRIANS IN THE GERMAN ARMY: A DIFFICULT TRANSITION FOR SOME

The added manpower of the Austrian military was the biggest asset that Hitler gained in the annexation of Austria. The two armies had a long-standing history of imperial alliances, and most of the Austrian military welcomed the opportunity to fight side by side with the German army. Of the 1.2 million Austrians who served in Hitler's armed forces, more than two hundred rose to the rank of general. By the war's end, 326 Austrians held Germany's highest military decoration, the Iron Cross—more than 40 of these earned it through service in the Waffen SS. The SS was Hitler's elite fighting group, which also committed some of the worst atrocities against civilians. Approximately 100,000 Austrians served in the SS.

However, not all of the Austrian military was quite so quick to embrace Nazism. Hitler recognized the fact and began systematically removing top officers and replacing them with his own handpicked leaders. Within a year, 55 percent of all Austrian generals and 40 percent of all colonels had been excluded from service in the German military. Even many of these old-time officers who stayed to serve in the new army were not happy with the changes in military philosophy. One, General Fred Payrleitner, expressed those feelings in his diary, which was quoted by Gordon Brook-Shepherd in *The Austrians: A Thousand-Year Odyssey*.

> We old-time officers had very different concepts implanted in us about the fulfilment of one's duty, about taking care of our soldiers, and the pleasure that came with a sense of responsibility. They are concepts which today still seem preferable to those principles of obedience and discipline which prevail in the German army. This sort of robot obedience will always be incomprehensible to any Austrian officer of the imperial school.

Party. Based on the report of the panel (known as the Three Wise Men) the EU then decided, in September 2000, to lift the sanctions imposed on Austria.

FOREIGNERS—FILLING A NEED OR TAKING AUSTRIAN JOBS?

Although Joerg Haider's stand on foreigners is extreme, many Austrians do believe that the influx of foreign workers creates a serious problem for Austria's economy. Since the 1960s, workers from poorer nations, such as the former Soviet bloc countries, have been drawn to Austria's affluence. By 1991 foreign workers made up more than 8 percent of the workforce—a fact that angers many Austrians. Historians Solsten and McClave write: "Although certain elements of the Austrian economy, especially hotels and restaurants, cannot function without foreign workers, many Austrians resent the employment of foreigners."[27]

To further complicate the issue, the EU recently announced that it was considering opening its membership to several former Soviet countries. As a result, large numbers of people are expected to emigrate in search of better jobs. Stefan Tissot is one Austian who believes that open borders are a good thing, but also that Austrian concerns are justified. He explains that although all EU countries will gain workers from Eastern Europe, Austria will be first: "Geographically, we will be the first stopping place for the immigrants. We fear that too many will choose to stay here rather than travel on. Our economy may not be able to absorb so many."[28]

Many Austrians share Tissot's fears and worry that, in addition to taking much-needed jobs away from Austrians, large numbers of immigrants could have a negative impact on the economy by overloading educational, health, and social systems. The Austrians say they struggled to build the strong economy they enjoy today and do not want to see it threatened.

ECONOMY—A REMARKABLE RECOVERY

Economists often call that sound, stable economy the Austrians built after World War II a model of recovery and economic growth. "*Klein aber fein*, or . . . 'small but beautiful'" is the way the editors of *Austria: A Country Study* describe Austria's economy. They go on to say, "Austria is a small European country in terms of gross domestic product [value of goods and services produced by the country], area, and population. Yet, since the end of World War II, it has achieved a remarkable record of growth, even when international conditions have not been at their most favorable."[29]

After World War II, Austria nationalized many industries, giving the government more control over economic activity. This policy and improvements in farming technology moved Austria's economy away from agriculture toward an emphasis on manufacturing products such as high-quality machinery, metals, textiles, and chemicals. These labor-intensive manufacturing industries now account for 75 percent of Austria's ex-

ports. Although the goods are sold all over the world, Germany and other Western European countries are the largest consumers. The nation also exports electricity generated by the abundant water supplies of the Alps to neighboring countries. These exports are crucial to Austria's economy because the nation, in return, depends on other countries to provide goods that are not made in Austria.

Since the end of World War II Austria has become a model of economic and industrial growth.

This trade with other countries is very important to Austria's economy. Therefore, the small nation has always supported trade agreements with neighboring countries and was a founding member of the European Free Trade Association, an organization formed in 1960 and supporting free trade among its member countries.

In spite of an increased export business, changes in technology and a shift to a more urban lifestyle have brought about a redistribution of the three major sectors of Austria's economy. The agricultural and industrial sectors have declined as the service sector has grown. Statistics show that in the 1970s industry and services, such as tourism, earned nearly equal shares of the gross domestic product. By 1990, however, the services

About 80 percent of Austria's land mass is used for farming and forestry.

share was twice that of industry. Agriculture's share has also fallen steadily, leaving services as the largest field of employment in the country.

AGRICULTURE: LESS LABOR, GREATER EFFICIENCY

The Austrian government has played a vital role in agriculture since World War II. After the war, food production was down all over Europe and little food was available on the international market. Hence, it was vitally important for Austria to be able to feed itself, so the government took steps such as providing subsidies (money for improving farming methods), setting price controls, and introducing new technology to revive agriculture.

Today, farm technology allows Austria to provide most of its own food with only 7 percent of the labor force employed in agriculture and forestry, compared to about 60 percent at the end of World War II. Furthermore about 80 percent of Austria's total land mass is used for farming and forestry. About half is forest and the rest is pasture and land suitable for planting crops. Field crops, meat, and dairy products account for the highest value in Austrian agricultural production.

INDUSTRY: QUALITY OVER QUANTITY

Increased farm efficiency allowed more Austrians to leave the land and turn to industry for employment. Austria's industry, which is spread throughout the nine provinces, has gained a global reputation for high standards of production and service. In the mountainous west, textile production is the principal industry; production of machinery, glass, electrical goods, and chemicals is centered in the eastern provinces. Heavy industry is located mainly near Vienna, and iron and steel production is concentrated around Linz in Upper Austria and Leoben in Styria.

Not only iron and steel, but metals and minerals of all types are important to Austria's economy. The metal industries make up the largest share of the nation's industrial output and form the basis for many other industries such as machine tool manufacturing, vehicle production, and factory construction. Additionally, Austria's mineral production has declined steadily in importance since World War II, but it is still a significant source of income in some mountainous areas.

SERVICE SECTOR: FOCUSED ON PEOPLE

In the late 1960s Austria's industry and services each employed about 47 percent of the workforce. By the late 1980s, however, the services share had grown to nearly 60 percent. Services, including such areas as retail trade, transportation, tourism, and money and banking, now employ the bulk of Austria's workforce.

Austria has several large retail chains, such as the grocery stores Billa and Spar Osterreich, that employ large numbers of people. However, most retail outlets are still small family owned and operated shops, especially in the rural villages.

Transportation is another service industry that employs a large number of people. An efficient transportation system connects Austria's cities and villages with each other and the rest of the world. Because of its central location, Austria plays an important role in the European rail network. A number of high-speed international trains pass through the country daily. Many Austrians travel from city to city on smaller state and privately owned rail lines. Automobile travel has also increased dramatically in recent decades, creating new jobs in automobile sales and servicing.

Despite gains in the retail trade and transportation, clean mountain air, panoramic views, clear blue lakes, and snow-covered slopes are Austria's most marketable resource. As a result, the greatest growth in service-related business has been in tourism. The Alps draw visitors from all over the world for skiing in winter and hiking and camping in summer. The largest tourist income comes from the alpine provinces of Tyrol, Vorarlberg, and Carinthia. However, the Salzkammergut is a favorite tourist destination in the summer, and cosmopolitan Vienna attracts visitors year round.

Austria houses its constant stream of tourists in more than twenty thousand hotels and guest houses, fifty thousand rooms in private homes, and many simpler accommodations such as youth hostels, mountain cabins, and campgrounds. Despite an influx of international chains, many smaller hotels are still family businesses.

Tourism has also brought about a boom in restaurants and entertainment events that cater to foreign visitors. In addition to traditional Austrian restaurants, international chains have opened restaurants—many serving American specialties such as hamburgers.

By far, tourism is Austria's largest service industry with the Alps attracting countless visitors every year.

WHAT FEET HAVE TROD THESE HALLS?

In 1390 the Hotel Goldener Adler in the old city of Innsbruck opened its doors to offer a dry bed and hearty meal to weary travelers. It has been catering to visitors in Tyrol ever since.

In its six-hundred-year history, the hotel claims to have offered respite to many illustrious travelers. According to a marble plaque, the hotel was a stopping point for Emperor Maximilian I, the young Mozart traveling with his father, Emperor Joseph II, the poet Johann Wolfgang von Goethe, King Ludwig II of Bavaria, the violinist Paganini, philosopher Jean Paul Sartre, writer Albert Camus, the poet Heinrich Heine, even U.S. astrounaut-turned-senator John Glenn.

The inn celebrated its six-hundreth anniversary in 1990 with extensive renovations that provide for the comfort of modern travelers without disturbing the charm of the past.

ENVIRONMENTAL QUANDARY

Tourism is key to the success of the Austrian economy, but tourism is also a major threat to the country's delicate mountain ecosystem. Once-quiet villages have grown to such an extent that some have as many as twenty hotel beds for each resident. Most of the tourists who sleep in those beds come to ski or participate in summer sports such as off-trail hiking and biking, all of which damage the forest. The Austrian government has, in recent years, tried to encourage ecologically sensitive forms of tourism, but the thrill of the slopes and the pleasures of boating and swimming in the mountain lakes are difficult for people to give up.

Tourism, however, is just one of several environmental threats facing Austria. For instance, traffic through the country has increased dramatically over the last thirty years. In 1992, 3.2 million private automobiles were registered to travel on twenty-two thousand kilometers (over thirteen thousand miles) of paved roads. But local traffic is not the biggest problem. Austria's central location makes it the most convenient route for thousands of large trucks that pass through the country transporting goods between other European nations. Air inversions (layers of warm air over cooler air) trap pollutants from those trucks in narrow valleys, causing damage to the mountain ecosystem.

*This superhighway
through Austria's
Brenner Pass has created
pollution problems due
to an increase in traffic.*

One of the most environmentally sensitive roads is the superhighway that runs from Germany across Austria's Tyrol province and through the Brenner Pass to Italy. Traffic on this road has increased from approximately 600,000 vehicles per year in the early 1970s to more than 10 million in the early 1990s. A fourth of that traffic consists of large trucks.

When Austria joined the EU in 1995, the union agreed that Austria could set quotas to limit the number of trucks traveling on its roads. In 1999, however, the quota was exceeded by 14 percent, and in June 2000 Austria threatened to take the issue to the EU's European Court of Justice.

Some Austrian people have become frustrated with the slow political process and have joined the fight against pollution by staging demonstrations. While the EU debated about the number of foreign trucks on Austria's highways, an environmental group blockaded the Brenner Pass road for thirty hours in a protest against the excessive traffic. This was the third such blockade in seven years.

The goal behind these protests is to stop further expansion of the roadway system in Austria and to force more cargo onto the railways. Some transport companies, for example, already transport their truck trailers on railroad cars through sensitive areas. Other solutions to the problem are being considered as well. For example, officials are considering building a tunnel under the Alps that would reach all the way from southern Germany to northern Italy.

Austria's weather systems and geographic placement are also culprits in environmental pollution. The editors of *Austria: A Country Study* write:

> Atlantic maritime weather systems carry pollution into Austria from northwestern Europe. Austria's proximity to industrialized regions of former Communist states, with negligible or no pollution control policies or equipment, combined with the influence of . . . weather systems, also has proved to be extremely harmful. Mediterranean weather systems transmit industrial pollutants from northern Italy.[30]

By the early 1990s, 37 percent of Austria's forests had been damaged by acid rain and vehicular and industrial pollutants. Not only does the forest damage affect tourism, but it

RECYCLE! IT'S THE LAW

Austrians are required by law to help protect their environment by recycling. Cans, paper, and plastic are collected by local authorities or can be deposited in recycling bins found on many city streets. Hazardous materials such as aerosol cans must be stored for collection twice a year, and many glass containers (especially beer bottles) have a return value. Returning bottles is simple at some grocery stores, where machines determine what type of bottle it is and how much money is due. The machine then prints out a voucher that can be applied toward groceries. It's the law, but most Austrians are proud of their clean, litter-free landscape and recycle willingly.

also increases the danger to villages of avalanches, erosion, mud slides, and flooding. The Austrian government is very sensitive to the problems of pollution and has introduced protections that include banning leaded gasoline, enforcing strict recycling laws, and promoting natural sources of energy such as wind and solar power.

Yet, for a small landlocked nation, internal controls are not enough. The nations surrounding Austria must also commit themselves to solving the pollution problem. Solsten and Mc-Clave write: "Part of the solution to Austria's ecological problem is being sought in stricter environmental legislation at the domestic level. Ultimately, however, pan-European and global cooperation in the realm of pollution and emission control will be necessary to protect the country's environment."[31]

Pollution is a problem that will not be easily solved, especially without international cooperation. Overall, the self-reliant Austrians have shown remarkable strength and ingenuity in converting the shattered infrastructure of a massive imperial conglomerate into the sound social and economic systems of a dynamic modern nation.

A LEGACY OF CULTURAL EXCELLENCE

The Habsburgs left a legacy not only for Austria but for the world to enjoy. The royal family never neglected the finer things of life and were largely responsible for the astounding musical brilliance that has been Austria's greatest gift to the world. They reveled in the pomp and ceremony of elegant court occasions and enjoyed fine art and music. In fact, several members of the royal family were musically talented. Leopold I, for example, was a composer; and Charles VI, Maria Theresa, and Joseph II were all accomplished musicians. Whether or not they played, they loved good music, good food, and grand occasions. One historian wrote of the royal family's love of festivity:

> the great cycles of ceremony revolved not only around the day of the Emperor, and the season, but around the rise and ebb [fall] of life itself. Christenings, marriages, coronations, funerals: all provided the occasion for the grand spectacle, the ceremonial gesture, the pageant in which theater and real life inextricably fused. The court was both spectator and participant. The great musicians of the day composed for the occasion; the great artists designed opera scenes, illuminations for the christenings, wedding festivals, coronation settings, and finally the catafalques [wooden frameworks] on which the imperial corpses were laid out.[32]

The Habsburg patronage of the arts allowed Austria, especially Vienna, to build an international reputation as a cultural center. Furthermore, Vienna embraced the arts and encouraged free expression and experimentation with new art forms, most notably new directions in music. In fact, three of the greatest composers in Europe during the late eighteenth and early nineteenth centuries (Franz Joseph Haydn, Wolfgang Amadeus Mozart, and Ludwig van Beethoven) lived and wrote their music in Austria.

PAPA HAYDN

Franz Joseph Haydn was born in 1732 to a poor family in Rohrau, Lower Austria. His father, a maker of wheels for horse-drawn carriages, was a talented harpist who sang Austrian folk songs to his children. He saw that Joseph had an exceptional musical talent and sent the boy to stay with a cousin where the youngster could study music. At eight years of age, Joseph's fine treble voice won him a place in Vienna's prestigious St. Stephen's Cathedral choir. By the time he was a teenager, he was composing his own music.

Haydn's brilliant compositions brought existing musical genres, or types, to new levels. According to the *Larousse Encyclopedia of Music:* "he is rightly known as the father of both the

Franz Joseph Haydn's gentle nature earned him the affectionate nickname, Papa Haydn.

string quartet and the symphony, not because he 'invented' them, but because in his hands they first reached their full stature."[33]

Besides composing and performing, Haydn spent many years as music director for the Esterhazy family on their estate in Burgenland. The Esterhazys were powerful and wealthy members of the Austrian nobility, a class of society just a step down from royalty. The family spent lavish amounts of money to encourage composers and musicians. While living on their estate, Haydn rehearsed, conducted the orchestra, and coached the singers and musicians under him. The kind and gentle composer was so popular with the younger musicians working for him that they fondly gave him the nickname Papa Haydn.

Haydn wrote *The Creation* and *The Seasons*, two great oratorios—musical compositions with a religious theme intended to be performed by singers and orchestra. In addition to these oratorios, he composed hundreds of other pieces including symphonies and music to be performed by string quartets, piano, and other instruments. He also met and offered guidance to some of the other great composers of the time. Ludwig van Beethoven, for example, studied under Haydn and in spite of musical disagreements they became fast friends. His closest friend, whom he considered almost like a son, was Wolfgang Mozart. Mozart once said of his friend and mentor, "He alone has the secret of making me smile, and touching me to the bottom of my soul."[34] Haydn died in 1809.

THE GIFTED CHILD

Wolfgang Amadeus Mozart (1756–1791) played for Austria's Empress Maria Theresa at Schonbrunn Palace when he was only six years old. His father wrote about the occasion:

> Their Majesties received us with such extraordinary graciousness that when I describe it, people will not believe me. Suffice it to say that Wolferl [an affectionate nickname] jumped upon the lap of the Empress, put his arms around her neck and kissed her heartily.[35]

By the time he entertained the empress, the precocious child had already been playing music for three years. When the young Mozart was still a toddler, his father, a court violinist and composer in Salzburg, recognized his son's exceptional gift.

Wolfgang Amadeus Mozart (foreground) was only six years old when he performed for the Empress Maria Theresa.

Wolfgang Mozart's older sister was also a talented musician, and their father took full advantage of his children's talents. They toured Europe, giving recitals everywhere they went.

Mozart soon learned that his greatest talent lay not in playing the music of others but in writing his own compositions. He wrote his first symphony when he was eight years old and his first opera at age twelve. Although he produced music in almost every genre, he is best known for his symphonies and operas including *The Marriage of Figaro, Don Giovanni,* and *The Magic Flute.*

In spite of his musical genius, Mozart never achieved the respect and financial success his work deserved. He and his wife Constance always had to struggle to make ends meet. Not only was he often underpaid, but his genius did not extend to the field of money management. When he died at age thirty-five, Mozart was buried in a pauper's grave in Vienna's Cemetery of

St. Mark. In his short lifetime, he gave the world more than six hundred musical compositions.

THE DEAF COMPOSER

Perhaps the most noted musician of the nineteenth century, Ludwig van Beethoven (1770–1827) was not Austrian by birth. However, he came from Germany to Austria for his musical education and spent most of his career in Vienna. Like Haydn and Mozart, he grew up in a musical family, but his mother became ill when he was young, thwarting his early plans to go to Vienna and study with Mozart. When Beethoven finally did make it to Vienna at the age of twenty-two, he was too late to study with Mozart, who had died the year before, but studied under Haydn and other noted Viennese musicians.

As a concert pianist, Beethoven was the darling of the fashionable society of Vienna. Yet his work was far from frivolous and his compositions made musical history. Among his best-known works are pieces such as the *Pastoral Symphony*, the opera *Fidelio*, and the *Ninth Symphony*.

German-born Ludwig van Beethoven studied music in Vienna under Haydn.

He did not lead a charmed life, however. Although he stayed in Vienna until his death, Beethoven never lived a stable life, moving as many as eighty times during those years. His love life was no more settled than his residence; he had many love affairs but never married. When he was not quite thirty years old, the brilliant young composer began showing signs of deafness. The condition progressed, and for the last ten years of his life Beethoven was completely deaf, yet he continued composing major masterpieces.

THE WALTZ

Haydn, Mozart, and Beethoven are the cornerstones of classical music, but Austria's musical heritage included dozens of other accomplished composers in every imaginable musical genre. In the early part of the nineteenth century, for example, a new form, lighter

than other music of the day, made its debut in Vienna. The waltz had its beginnings in Austria's ethnic folk music but gained polish and sophistication in Vienna. The joyful airy style of the new music, and the dance steps that went with it, grabbed the imagination of the people, and soon everyone was waltzing. Composers Johann Strauss and Josef Lanner made the waltz popular, but it was Strauss's son Johann Baptist Strauss who brought it to full flower. Among the four hundred waltzes he composed are *The Blue Danube* and *Tales From the Vienna Woods*.

The waltz as a dance was not instantly embraced by all. Dance teachers saw it as a threat to their profession because dancers could easily master the basic steps. The waltz also faced criticism on moral grounds. Religious leaders called the close hold and rapid turning movements vulgar and sinful. However, the joy of the new dance could not be dampened, and the waltz soon spread beyond Austria to the rest of Europe and the United States.

The waltz is still popular around the world, but outside Austria musicians tend to speed up the tempo, perhaps a result of today's fast-paced way of life. Professor Edward Strauss, con-

Couples dance to the waltz made popular by Austrian composers Johann Strauss, Johann Baptist Strauss, and Josef Lanner.

UGLY DUCKLING OR BELOVED LANDMARK?

Many people think the grandiose Vienna State Opera House is hardly distinguishable from the other ornate buildings on the Ringstrasse. Yet, when it was completed in 1869, the Viennese were so ruthless in their criticism of it that one of the architects, Eduard van der Null, committed suicide.

The building remained unpopular with many Viennese until 1945, when American bombers aiming for industrial targets across the Danube bombed the opera house, leaving it a burned-out shell. This bombing could have given the Viennese their long-awaited chance to rebuild it in a more popular style. However, they did not seize the opportunity. Instead, all of Vienna rejoiced when the stately opera house reopened in 1955, restored to look exactly as it had before.

The Vienna State Opera House.

ductor and grandnephew of Johann Strauss said in an interview with writer Peter White: "A lot of people today play the waltz too fast. The waltz is an embodiment of liveliness, and many people think this means speed. But liveliness has nothing to do with speed. When people lived at a slower pace, they were just as lively as today, and they enjoyed things more."[36]

MUSIC TODAY

Today music is still an integral part of Austrian life and is as varied as the people. People flock to the state opera house or to

concert halls for performances of classical and other musical
styles. The Vienna Boys' Choir, an institution since 1498, still
sings every Sunday in the Royal Chapel in the Hofburg (Imperial Palace) and also tours and sings all over the world.

Folk and ethnic music are also popular in Austria, especially
in rural areas. The lively wine taverns of Vienna have their own
musical tradition in which tavern bands play folk and patriotic
music. Throughout Austria, provincial villages still celebrate
their ethnic culture with the music of their ancestors. Today,
Austrians also enjoy the international influence of modern
musical forms such as rock and jazz.

In an article for *National Geographic*, Peter T. White writes
about the Austrian and in particular the Viennese devotion to
music:

> Through the city's ups and downs, extraordinary enthusi-
> asm for music has survived. Where but in Vienna—and I
> have this on excellent authority—would Soviet Intelli-
> gence try to make friends and influence junior officials by
> offering them good seats at the opera?[37]

PROSE AND VERSE

Although the nation reached extraordinary artistic heights
with its musical achievements, Austrians are also well repre-
sented in other art forms. Its literary heritage began in the Middle Ages with works such as the *Nibelungenlied* (Song of the
Nibelungs) by an unknown author. German composer Richard
Wagner later interpreted this epic poem of passion and re-
venge into an operatic series.

In later years Austria's literary contributions were solid, if not
as brilliant as its musical accomplishments. The country has
produced some excellent playwrights and novelists. For example, during the nineteenth century several Austrian playwrights
made a lasting impact on the theater, most notably Franz Grillparzer (1791–1872). Grillparzer's many tragedies and historical
dramas are best known for their psychological insight and are
still performed today. During the same period Adalbert Stifter
wrote idealistic novels such as *Indian Summer* (1857), exploring
the search for a just and peaceful life.

At the beginning of the twentieth century, writers and artists
throughout Europe were pushing the limits of tradition and exploring new forms of expression. Austrian writer Karl Kraus, for

example, experimented with using interviews and newspaper accounts to tell his story in *The Last Days of Mankind.* Poet Peter Altenberg recorded the lives of the bohemian, or unconventional, people of Vienna. Austria's contemporary literature followed a similar style and includes the prose and stylistic plays of Peter Handke, the novels of Elfriede Jelinek, and the poetry of Friederike Mayrocker.

ART AND ARCHITECTURE

Much of the early art of Europe, including that of Austria, had a religious theme. Austria followed the trends of Europe,

ST. STEPHEN'S CATHEDRAL: A NEVER-ENDING PROJECT

In 1147 a bishop traveling with an army of the Second Crusade consecrated a new church outside the walls of the village of Vienna. The church of St. Stephen's has been under construction ever since.

As fashion and technology have changed, so has the church. About a century after construction on the original church began, an impressive Romanesque entrance was built. It is flanked by two octagonal towers that date to the earliest construction. In the 1200s the church was twice nearly destroyed by fire; each time, it was rebuilt.

As Vienna grew, the church became too small. Additions made during the late 1300s were Gothic in style and are still among the finest examples of Gothic architecture in Austria. The 450-foot-tall south tower, a Gothic masterpiece, remains the symbolic center of the city.

In the final days of World War II, the cathedral caught fire from flying sparks from nearby bombed buildings. The damage was extensive: Even the cathedral's great bell fell and shattered on the floor of the church.

No other structural loss was as painful to the people of Vienna as their great church. But St. Stephen's became a symbol of starting over again. Citizens from all over Austria helped remove the wreckage and rebuild the cathedral. Each province made a contribution as well. The new bell, the largest free-swinging bell in Europe, came from Upper Austria, the gate from Styria, and the stone floor from Lower Austria. The pews were made in Vorarlberg and the windows in Tyrol. The chandeliers came from Carinthia, and the communion rail from Burgenland; the province of Salzburg contributed the tabernacle; and Vienna paid for the elaborate tile roof to be restored.

The Schloss Belvedere (shown) is a popular example of eighteenth-century baroque architecture.

adding its own innovations to each style, and boasts some outstanding examples of religious ideas expressed both in architecture and the fine arts. Since religion was the central theme, great churches were built, and elaborate art and sculpture were created to decorate them. For example, thick walls and heavy rounded arches characterize the Romanesque, or Roman-inspired, churches of the Babenberg dynasty (976–1246). These churches usually included sculpture in the form of ornate doors or decorative supporting columns, paintings of biblical scenes and abstract patterns on church walls, and wall designs of mosaics—arrangements of bits of colored tile.

In the 1100s new technology in building construction brought changes in architectural styles, and Romanesque gave way to Gothic. Gothic designs included thinner walls, more delicate features, and large ornate windows. The large Gothic windows opened the way to stained glass as an elaborate new art form. Vienna's St. Stephen's Cathedral, in spite of being a mix of styles, is the finest example of Gothic architecture in Austria.

BAROQUE ARCHITECTURE

Although Austria has many excellent examples of early architectural styles, no art or architectural form affected the appearance of its cities as much as the Baroque style of the seventeenth and eighteenth centuries. Baroque architecture is characterized by a sense of movement and energy with strong contrasts of light and shadow. Baroque buildings with their curving walls and ornate surface decoration imply the same feeling of motion and life that can be seen in the paintings and sculptures of the era.

The Baroque style became popular in Austria during the rebuilding period after the Thirty Years' War (1618–1648) that ended the Protestant Reformation and brought Catholicism back into dominance in Austria. There was renewed emphasis on religion, and both the emperor and the church contributed to the popularity of the rich ornamentation and gold decoration of the Baroque style.

Although Baroque originated in Italy, Austrian architect Johann Bernhard Fischer von Erlach (1656–1723) used the postwar rebuilding period to develop it into the national style of Austria. Von Erlach made his Baroque designs uniquely Austrian through dynamic combinations of color blended with irregular or curving lines. Two cathedrals designed by von Erlach, the Kollegienkirche in Salzburg and the Karlskirche in Vienna, are among Austria's most outstanding examples of Baroque architecture.

THE RISE OF SECULAR ART

Gradually artists began combining landscapes and other subject matter with religious art until purely secular (nonreligious) art became popular. One of Austria's best-known secular artists was Gustav Klimt, who worked in the late 1800s and early 1900s—a time of intellectual excitement in Vienna. New ideas about art, philosophy, and life were being freely expressed during this period, and just as freely rejected by conservatives. Klimt was a leader in expressing changing ideas through his art. According to art historians, his work "embodies the high-keyed erotic, psychological, and aesthetic preoccupations of turn-of-the-century Vienna's dazzling intellectual world."[38]

Austrian artists Gustav Klimt (shown) and Otto Wagner started the Secession Movement.

Klimt was a successful decorative and mural painter working in a highly symbolic style until the mid-1890s, when he began to see art as a more personal form of expression. In 1897 he and artist-architect Otto Wagner brought together other architects and artists who refused to conform to the standards of the past and started the Secession Movement (sometimes called art nouveau). The Secessionists expressed themselves through rich colors, sensuous curving lines, and floral motifs. Their themes often expressed sexuality and were seen as decadent and excessive by more conservative members of society. Klimt, in particular, created major scandals with his erotic, symbolic murals. Under the leadership of Klimt and Wagner, the Secessionists published a journal, held exhibitions, and in the early 1900s built their own exhibition hall. The Secession Hall, topped by an intricate gold dome, still stands in Vienna as a monument to artistic freedom.

PRESERVING THE OLD

Despite major damage inflicted by two world wars, Austria retains many fine examples of architecture from a grander era, and as a result Austria's cities have become a blend of old and new. The clean stark lines of modern architecture emphasize the ornate appeal of the old. But many cities have preserved their oldest sections and allow no modern structures in those old towns. The narrow winding streets of the old towns are often closed to vehicular traffic and have become magnets for tourists. *Old* is a relative term, however, and even outside the designated old towns much of the architecture is often aged and ornate.

During the latter half of the twentieth century, Austrians began placing great emphasis on preserving the old, sometimes at the expense of growth and progress in the modern world. This preservation policy focuses on protecting the historical value of old buildings and making sure that new additions conform to the form, style, and overall appearance of the old. Interest in preservation began as early as the nineteenth century but experienced a boom period in the 1960s and 1970s when several preservation action groups stepped up their advocacy for preservation.

Austrian state law prohibits any alterations to historic property without a permit. Not everyone supports this policy, however. And sometimes frustrated property owners resort to illegal means to renovate their property, such as doing the work secretly or bribing officials. This dilemma raises some difficult but as yet unanswered questions for the preservationists, as author Sabina Wiedenhoeft points out:

> While recognition of a rich and diverse cultural tradition worth preserving is shared by most Austrians, the tremendous focus and government funding of preservation has begun to be questioned. Are Austrian cities losing a modern identity at the expense of preserving the old? Are historic buildings really being preserved as cul-

EQUINE BALLET

In 1562 Emperor Maximilian II brought several dancing Lipizzaner stallions to Austria, and for more than four hundred years since, the horses have been captivating audiences with their elegant moves. The horses perform their equine ballet at the Spanish Riding School in Vienna. Bred on a stud farm in Styria under the watchful eye of the Ministry of Agriculture, Lipizzaner stallions are born a dark grayish brown and take five to twelve years to change to the distinctive white color. Each year about five stallions are selected from the forty or so foals born on the farm. They are sent to the school in Vienna to begin years of rigorous training; it takes two years for them to learn just the distinctive Lipizzaner style of walking with its high-knee action and stately vertical carriage.

In his article, "The White Horses of Vienna," *National Geographic* writer Beverley Bowie described the dance of the elegant white stallions as "an art form of great subtlety and power, as abstract and as moving as the ballet." Once their training is complete the stallions perform their elegant moves, accompanied by classical music, in the school's ornate hall with arched windows and crystal chandeliers.

A trainer walks a Lipizzaner stallion during a horse show.

tural artifacts or simply as tourist Meccas? How many monuments can realistically be preserved . . . . Another concern facing Austrian preservation today is the integration of historic buildings with modern ones.[39]

FESTIVALS

Austria preserves its less tangible heritage through frequent festivals that celebrate its long history of folk art and music. Each province preserves its own native costumes, crafts, and history through local festivals, and all of Austria glories in this venue for celebrating its musical history. Most festivals are outdoor events held in the warm weather of spring and summer. Some are large internationally known extravaganzas drawing visitors from all over the world.

Since its beginning in 1920, the Salzburg Festival has grown until many consider it the world's most renowned musical and theatrical event. The music of Mozart, a native of Salzburg, has always been the central theme of the festival. However, the more than 175 festival events present an array of theatrical and musical selections from Mozart classics to contemporary compositions.

Another festival, the Bregenz Festival in the province of Vorarlberg, includes a wide range of operas, orchestral works, and theatrical productions featuring international performers. Performances take place on the Seebuhne—a huge, open-air floating stage on the edge of Lake Constance. The event is so popular that tickets must be purchased about nine months in advance.

At any time of the year, music fans can find some type of special musical event in Vienna, but the favorite for both the Viennese and visitors is the Vienna Festival held from mid-May to mid-June. The festival presents a varied arts program in concert halls and theaters around the city. In 2000 the festival included such diverse events as a performance of Beethoven's collected symphonies; a presentation of *The Seagull,* a comedy by Russian writer Anton Chekhov; and a pop-music fairy tale version of *Peter Pan.*

The love of music and the arts has been a unifying force in Austria. Through the centuries, the country has faced war and peace, power and obscurity, poverty and affluence, but through it all the sound of music has filled the air.

FINDING A NATIONAL IDENTITY

6

Much has been written about Austria's lack of a national identity, and it is true that these people began as a mixed bag of diverse cultures. The wanderers of Europe poured into this crossroads region from many different backgrounds. They did not join together as a new nation but formed tight little communities—each keeping a wary eye on its neighbors.

As a group of small communities, they became important not because of who they were but because of where they were. Their position was strategic to the defense of Europe from invaders from the east. Author Gordon Brook-Shepherd explains that: "The Austrians of the future thus entered history not as a tribal (let alone national) entity, but as a geographical concept."[40]

From the beginning, they were battered by the winds of political change and unstable boundaries. They found stability in seeing themselves as Tyrolean, Styrian, or Viennese rather than Austrian. When they had to identify with a larger world, they saw themselves as German.

A GERMANIC BOND

In the early days of Europe, the term *German* referred to a shared language and similar background, not to a geographic or political unit. There were many German tribes, and most of the inhabitants of what is now Austria descended from these early German peoples. They spoke German and related to German culture. The Holy Roman Empire was a German invention.

Nevertheless, under the Habsburgs the wealth and power of the empire rested in Austrian lands, and the emperors built their seat of government and their homes there. Still, the Austrian people did not build a sense of themselves as a nation. The Habsburgs, after all, ruled not just Austria but a vast empire of mostly small Germanic states. Austria's position as the

DRESSING UP

Generally, Austrians, especially the Viennese, are indistinguishable from people in any major city in the world. Not only is their style of clothing international, but many of the same name brands popular in New York, London, or Berlin can be seen in store windows and on the streets of Austria's cities.

However, many people, especially in rural communities, delight in dressing in the traditional clothing of their province for festivals and special occasions. And for some, especially in small farming communities, dirndls (mountain-style jumpers) and lederhosen (men's leather shorts with suspenders) are still daily attire. In the mountain provinces, shops feature a wide variety of traditional dress, especially lederhosen, and the delicately embroidered aprons and kerchiefs of Tyrol.

An innkeeper in native Austrian dress.

seat of Habsburg rule overshadowed its identity as a nation, and Austrians saw themselves simply as part of the mosaic of German states.

Brook-Shepherd writes of an unknown eighteenth-century artist in the duchy of Styria who produced a painting titled *Short Description of the Peoples of Europe, Together with Their Characteristics.* Ten images of leaders in national costumes represent the major nations of Europe of the day; underneath is a list of their national characteristics. Surprisingly, the painting, although Austrian in origin, did not include an Austrian leader.

> [T]he oddest (and most significant) thing of all to modern eyes about this *Table of Peoples* [the painting], as it became known, was something which evidently appeared perfectly natural to the artist. Though he was a subject of the Austrian Monarchy—living indeed in one of the oldest hereditary lands of the "Casa Austria"—there is no mention of Austrians [in the painting] among the ten nations of his Europe. They are simply subsumed under one composite heading, "The Germans."[41]

The creation of the Austro-Hungarian dual monarchy in 1867 only added to the ethnic confusion. Austrians felt a strong cultural bond with their German neighbors but were politically welded to their non-German speaking neighbors to the southeast. When World War I brought the collapse of the Habsburg dynasty and the breakup of the dual monarchy, most Austrians doubted that a small German-speaking state could survive on its own. They saw two possibilities: membership in a confederation of the states formed out of the Austro-Hungarian dual monarchy or unification with Germany. However, the treaties signed at the end of the war prohibited unification, and efforts to unite the nations of the former monarchy in a confederation failed.

Austria was cast out on its own to sink or swim as a nation. The years between the wars were difficult. So when native Austrian Adolf Hitler's army marched into Austria, many Austrians welcomed annexation to Germany and saw it as the solution to their country's economic and political problems. As it turned out, it was the annexation that pushed the Austrian people to see themselves as members of a distinct nation with its own consciousness and identity. According to Solsten and McClave:

Since World War II, Austrians have carved out a national identity separate and distinct from their German neighbors.

[Following the annexation] Austrians increasingly focused on the historical and cultural differences between Austrian and German traditions—or the uniqueness and singularity of an "Austrian nation"—and on the idea of an independent Austrian state. It is one of those quirks of history that the experience of being "German" in the Third Reich was instrumental in awakening feelings of Austrian nationalism for many Austrians, who, by the end of World War II, wholeheartedly endorsed the idea of Austrian independence from Germany. This idea involved rejecting the concept of one "German-speaking linguistic and cultural nation" for the sake of two German-speaking nations: one German and the other Austrian.[42]

Austria emerged from World War II still facing overwhelming problems, but with a new national identity. Austrians today take pride in their nation. They cherish their mixed cultural heritage, and each province takes care to preserve its uniqueness. But overall, they see themselves as part of the whole—as Austrians.

THE NEW AUSTRIANS

Since 1955, when Austria won its independence from four-power rule, it has evolved into a highly developed democratic state offering a wide range of social security and health care benefits to its people. The Austrians have formed an open, democratic, socially mobile, prosperous government and society with few class distinctions. And as a neutral nation between the East and the West, they have built a vital position in the European community.

Modern Austrians enjoy a high standard of living. In the early 1990s, their quality of life was rated the world's tenth best by Washington's Population Crisis Committee, a group that does comparative studies of populations and lifestyles. They have built on the Habsburg legacy of keen appreciation of music, the arts, and a sophisticated and cultured lifestyle. Fine cars, sleek boats, fashionable clothing, and the ever-present cell phone are trademarks of the mostly middle-class society. Furthermore, most Austrians are multilingual with a sound general education and specialization in a vocational or professional field.

EDUCATION

Free public education, including a fine college, technical school, and university system, is available to all Austrian citizens. Though the system is free, it has not always offered equal opportunity for all because parents usually choose for their children the same type of education they themselves received.

All Austrian children attend elementary school (*Volksschule*) from the ages of six to ten. Then the school system splits into two tracks, and students or their parents have to choose the type of higher school they will attend. Because the children are so young, the parents usually make that decision. Austrian students may enroll in either a four-year middle school (*Hauptschule*) or an eight-year university preparatory gymnasium (*Allgemein-bildende Hoher Schule* [AHS]). After *Hauptschule*, students are required to take at least one year of vocational training, and AHS students have the option of going to a university.

Before the 1960s, the education system formed a self-perpetuating class system. Agricultural, lower-, and middle-

class families tended to send their children to *Hauptschule;* the children from middle-class backgrounds were more likely to follow *Hauptschule* with extended vocational training. It was mostly wealthy and professional-level parents who chose to send their children to an AHS to prepare for a university education.

Reforms begun in the early 1960s, however, have given the system more flexibility, allowing students to make career decisions at a later age and offering more opportunity to change their minds later in their education. All state-funded schools are open to all Austrian residents regardless of birth, gender, race, status, class, language, or religion. The goal is to make higher education an equal opportunity for all.

Results of these reforms can be seen in the changing enrollment in Austria's twelve universities and six academies of music and art. In the mid-1960s, less than 10 percent of all students completed the AHS track, and more than 66 percent of those who did were male. By the early 1990s, however, more than 30 percent of all students were completing the AHS track,

Reforms implemented during the early 1960s provided Austrian students more flexibility in making decisions on higher education.

and a little more than 50 percent of them were female. Changes in the law also made it possible for some students without an AHS degree to enroll in a university.

But the system is not perfect. Classism and sexism continue to pose problems. In the early 1990s, children of white-collar workers, civil servants, and professionals still made up more than 80 percent enrollment in institutions of higher education, and despite the great increase in female college and university enrollments, women have not taken an equal role in the workplace. For example, in 1990, only 2 percent of university professors were women.

VIENNA'S BIG WHEEL

The giant Ferris wheel of Prater Park is one of the most familiar landmarks of Vienna. The wheel was built in 1896 and 1897 as part of the celebration of Emperor Franz Joseph's fiftieth year as emperor.

Fifteen enclosed cabins lift visitors almost two hundred feet into the air for a breathtaking view of the city. The view is so good that in World War I the military took over the wheel as a lookout point. In World War II it fell victim to Allied bombing and fire, but in 1947 the badly damaged wheel was reconstructed and has been in constant operation since.

In war and peace, the great wheel has had an exciting existence. It has served as a revolving stage for performances and publicity stunts. For example, in 1914 Madame Solange D'Atalide, a circus performer and horsewoman, rode the wheel astride a horse standing atop one of the cabins.

One cabin was renovated in 1987 as a luxury cabin, complete with mahogany paneling, art nouveau curtains, carpeting, and modern lighting systems. The

luxury cabin is available for special occasion rentals at a cost of approximately $250 per hour. Less wealthy riders can, for a very small fee, take a spin in one of the other cabins and enjoy a stunning view that has drawn thrill seekers for more than one hundred years.

After two world wars, the giant Prater Park Ferris wheel still spins.

TIME TO PLAY

Life is not all work and school in Austria. A healthy economy allows time for a wide variety of leisure activities. Most Austrians are drawn to the outdoors because their country's geography provides exceptional opportunities for outdoor recreation. In cold weather, Austrians mingle with thousands of foreigners on the ski slopes for both alpine and cross-country skiing. During the warmer months, boating, swimming, and diving are favorite pastimes, particularly in the lakes of the Salzkammergut, and the warm waters of the Neusiedler See, a large shallow lake in Burgenland.

There are also hundreds of miles of bicycle trails through scenic landscapes. Most follow the more level terrain along shores of lakes and rivers, but there are rigorous mountain trails as well. Because bicycling is almost a national pastime, some railway cars and buses have special sections for transporting bicycles; most streets have separate bike tracks; and many train stations rent bikes that can be returned to any other train station with a rental office.

A VARIED CUISINE

Dining out is an enjoyable pastime for Austrians. The choice of styles in food and restaurants is almost endless. Austria has a worldwide reputation for delectable pastries and cakes—as beautiful as they are delicious. Pastries are most often served in a coffee house with an espresso, a cup of gold (more milk than coffee), a small brown one (a small cup with slightly more coffee than milk), or any number of other coffee varieties.

Austria's more substantial culinary offerings reflect the heritage of the provinces, and even of the invaders and travelers who passed through over the centuries. Sausages and cheeses; an infinite variety of breads, noodles, and dumplings; dishes richly seasoned with paprika and garlic; delicately steamed fish; and succulent vegetables are all part of the daily fare. Austria took the best dishes of Germany, Eastern Europe, Russia, and Italy, gave them a special Austrian twist, and made them its own.

Dining atmosphere is as varied as the food. The corner *imbiss* (snack bar) offers bratwurst (sausage) and *pommes frites* (french fries) to munch on in transit or on a nearby bench. At the other extreme are elegant, but usually cozy, restaurants with heavy draperies, antique furnishings, fresh flowers, and white linen on the tables. More casual sit-down dining can be

VIENNESE COFFEEHOUSES

When Vienna's first coffeehouse opened in 1685, the people of Vienna fell in love with the idea and adopted it as a way of life. Today Austrians drink more coffee than any other beverage—221 liters (about sixty-six gallons) per person per year. Beer, the second most popular beverage, falls way behind coffee at only 120 liters (thirty-six gallons) per person, and the wine that the nation is known for brings up the rear at a mere 33 liters (about ten gallons) per person.

Coffeehouses often have outdoor seating where patrons can watch the world go by. Many offer a selection of magazines and newspapers for patrons to enjoy as they sip their favorite coffee, and some provide musical entertainment. Austria actually has two types of coffeehouses, although the distinction between the two is blurring. The *Kaffeehaus*, usually preferred by men, offers games such as billiards and chess, and often serves light meals and alcoholic beverages as well as coffee. A *Café Konditorei* is patronized more by women; it typically has more elegant decor and specializes in cakes and pastries. Whether the choice is a lively *Kaffeehaus* or a sophisticated *Konditorei*, at four o'clock most Austrians stop to linger over coffee.

Patrons in Vienna's coffee houses may linger while enjoying their coffee and pastries.

found at wine taverns, beer gardens, and other establishments with wooden tables and noisy chatter.

WHERE AUSTRIANS LIVE

Most Austrians in big cities live in large apartment buildings or in apartments that occupy the top floors over shops. City dwellers manage to bring a bit of the outdoors to their homes with flower boxes at their windows. Suburbs and villages, on the other hand, are crowded with neat two-story houses surrounded by colorful, well-kept flower and vegetable gardens. And the people there also decorate their windows and balconies with bright boxes of petunias and geraniums. Steeply peaked roofs provide for extra attic living space and prevent a heavy buildup of snow. In mountain farming areas, families often live above the barn, an innovation that came about because of the difficulty of getting through deep snows to tend to livestock. Even with a barn downstairs, rural houses are neat, clean, and colorful.

Although the charming alpine building styles have not changed much over the centuries, housing has changed radically since World War II. Following the war, there was a serious housing shortage and most homes lacked running water and indoor plumbing. Since then, living units have increased by well over 50 percent, even though the population has increased by only about 10 percent. New houses almost always have modern conveniences, and most old ones have been renovated to incorporate modern plumbing. Less than 10 percent of living units lack these facilities today.

Austrian homes have steeply peaked roofs to provide attic space and allow runoff of heavy snows.

More than 55 percent of all Austrians own their own homes or apartments either privately or as a part of ownership cooperatives; additionally almost 10 percent of Austrians own a second residence used for recreational purposes. These range from garden plots with tiny cottages to spacious single-family homes in the country.

GRAND HOUSES OF WORSHIP AND CRUMBLING ATTENDANCE

The homes of most Austrians are comfortable and unpretentious, but their houses of worship are likely to be elegant and heavily ornamented. In fact, Austria's Baroque and Gothic architects found their grandest expression in cathedrals and churches. Even the smallest villages have one or more places of worship, usually the most ornate and lavish building in the community. Austrians take pride in the architecture and rich decor of their churches. However, the

AN EVENING AT THE *HEURIGER*

A relaxing evening at a *Heuriger* (wine tavern) is a treasured tradition among Austrians. The word *Heuriger* means wine from the last harvest, but it also means a tavern that serves the wine. A typical *Heuriger* has both inside and outside seating and a relaxed jovial atmosphere. Wandering musicians, often a guitarist and an accordion player, provide entertainment. It is a place for the whole family, even children and the family dog, to spend an evening talking, eating, drinking wine, and greeting old friends.

Vienna's *Heurigen* are located in the city's Grinsing district near the vineyards and belong to the vineyard owners. Originally they served no food, although it was perfectly acceptable for patrons to bring their own food. Today, the *Heurigen* serve food but do not provide table service.

In recent years tourists discovered the *Heurigen*, and many taverns could not meet the growing demand for wine without supplementing their supplies with outside wines. However, hidden in the narrow back alleys of Grinsing where few tourists manage to find their way, there are still true *Heurigen*. These taverns serve only the fresh tart wine from their own vineyards. A fresh green bough hanging in front of a light over the door sends the message that the harvest is in and wine is being served. Traditionally, a pitcher of wine is served with a pitcher of sparkling water, and patrons mix the two about half and half. The combination makes a cool refreshing drink and delivers no hangover the next day.

Heurigen *are popular gathering places for good conversation, music, and wine tasting.*

In the years since the Protestant Reformation, 80 percent of Austrians reverted to Catholicism.

position of the church as a center of spiritual and social life is declining.

Austria has traditionally been a Roman Catholic state, with close ties between church and government. Through most of the Habsburg dynasty, life centered around the doctrines of the church and the society of the parish. Even though many Austrians abandoned Catholicism for Protestantism during the Reformation, in the years that followed they reverted to Catholicism. And today, most of the population professes to be Catholic. According to the 1991 census, almost 80 percent of Austrians belong to the Catholic Church.

However, the role the church plays in their lives has diminished over the years. Recently, Austrians, though still Catholic,

have become increasingly less conservative. Solsten and Mc-
Clave report that:

> The influence of the Roman Catholic Church, although
> still formidable because of its historical position in Aus-
> trian society . . . receded in the postwar period. The form
> of nominal Roman Catholicism many Austrians practice
> is called "baptismal certificate Catholicism." In other
> words, most Roman Catholics observe traditional reli-
> gious holidays, such as Christmas and Easter, and rely
> on the church to celebrate rites of passage, such as bap-
> tisms, confirmations, weddings, and funerals, but do
> not participate actively in parish life or follow the teach-
> ings of the Roman Catholic Church on central issues.
> This trend can be seen in the low rate of regular church
> attendance (less than one-third of Catholics) and the
> high rates of divorce and abortion in the 1980s and early
> 1990s.[43]

INTO THE NEW MILLENNIUM

The role of religion is not the only thing that is changing in
modern Austria. According to Anton Pelinka, Austria enters
the twenty-first century less distinctive than it once was. Austria has moved away from many of the things that made it dis-
tinctly Austrian and has become more like other modern
nations:

> The future has already begun. And this future is open—
> with regard to electoral results, to the party system, to
> parliament and government, to social conflicts and po-
> litical attitudes. But there is a blueprint for the future:
> Whatever form the new Austria will take, it will be less
> Austrian and more European, less distinctive and more
> similar to other European countries.[44]

In terms of politics, economy, and lifestyle, Europe is becoming more homogenized, meaning each country is becoming more like the others in character and culture. And it is true
that Austria is adjusting to fit this new European image. However, the things that make Austria unique are resistant to
change. The nation's varied heritage, pride in the land's majestic beauty, and the capital city's international reputation for sophistication and cultural innovation have had a lasting effect

on the way Austrians see themselves—and on the image they present to the world. Whatever the future brings, the name *Austria* will always evoke memories of imperial grandeur and royal pomp and ceremony. It will also stand as a reminder of overwhelming challenges faced and overcome. And Austria's phenomenal musical heritage will continue to lift the spirits of the world.

FACTS ABOUT AUSTRIA

THE GOVERNMENT

Official name: (English long form)- Republic of Austria; (Local long form)- Republik Osterreich

Government type: Federal republic

Capital: Vienna

Flag: Red/white/red equal size horizontal stripes

National Anthem: *Land der Berge, Land am Stroem* [Land of Mountains, Land of the River]

THE LAND

Land boundaries: Total: 2,562 km

Border countries: Czech Republic 362 km, Germany 784 km, Hungary 366 km, Italy 430 km, Liechtenstein 35 km, Slovakia 91 km, Slovenia 330 km, Switzerland 164 km

Area: Total: 83,858 sq km; Land: 82,738 sq km; Water: 1,120 sq km

Climate: temperate; continental, cloudy; cold winters with frequent rain in lowlands and snow in mountains; cool summers with occasional showers

Terrain: in the west and south mostly mountains (Alps); along the eastern and northern margins mostly flat or gently sloping

Elevation extremes: Lowest point: Neusiedler See 115 m

Highest point: Grossglockner 3,797 m

Natural resources: iron ore, oil, timber, magnesite, lead, coal, lignite, copper, hydropower

Land use: Arable land: 17%; Permanent pastures: 23%; Permanent crops: 1%; Forests and woodland: 39%; Other: 20% (1996 est.)

Environment—current issues: some forest degradation caused by air and soil pollution; soil pollution results from the use of agricultural chemicals; air pollution results from emissions by coal- and oil-fired power stations and industrial plants and from trucks transiting Austria between northern and southern Europe

THE PEOPLE:

Population growth rate: 0.009% (1999 est.)

Birth rate: 9.62 births/1,000 population (1999 est.)

Death rate: 10.04 deaths/1,000 population (1999 est.)

Age structure: 0–14 years: 17% (male 702,261; female 666,310); 15–64 years: 68% (male 2,792,484; female 2,713,397); 65 years and over: 15% (male 478,071; female 786,776) (1999 est.)

Languages: German

AUSTRIA: SIZE AND POPULATION

Province	Capital	Size (in sq. km)	Population (in thousands)
Burgenland	Eisenstadt	4,966	274.8
Carinthia	Klagenfurt	9,533	562.2
Lower Austria	St. Polten	19,173	1,521.5
Upper Austria	Linz	11,980	1,383.8
Salzburg	Salzburg	7,154	508.4
Styria	Graz	16,388	1207.8
Tyrol	Innsbruck	12,648	659.9
Vorarlberg	Bregenz	2,601	343.8
Vienna	Vienna	415	1,592.6
Austria	Vienna	83,857	8,054.8

NOTES

INTRODUCTION: A LAND OF CONTRADICTIONS

1. Anton Pelinka, *Austria: Out of the Shadow of the Past.* Boulder, CO: Westview Press, 1998, p. xi.

CHAPTER 1: A CULTURAL MOSAIC

2. Austrian Press and Information Service, "Lower Austria." www.austria.org/llower.htm.

3. Austrian Press and Information Service, "Tyrol." www. austria.org/ltyrol.htm.

CHAPTER 2: BUILDING A DYNASTY

4. Dorothy Gies McGuigan, *The Habsburgs.* New York: Doubleday, 1966, p. 3.

5. Quoted in McGuigan, *The Habsburgs,* p. 3.

6. Gordon Brook-Shepherd, *The Austrians: A Thousand-Year Odyssey.* New York: Carrol & Graf, 1996, p. 11.

7. Quoted in Brook-Shepherd, *The Austrians,* p. 13.

8. Brook-Shepherd, *The Austrians,* p. 14.

9. Brook-Shepherd, *The Austrians,* p. 15.

10. Edward Crankshaw, *The Habsburgs: Portrait of a Dynasty.* New York: Viking Press, 1971, p. 155.

11. Quoted in Crankshaw, *The Habsburgs,* p. 168.

12. Quoted in Crankshaw, *The Habsburgs,* p. 230.

13. Gordon Brook-Shepherd, *Archduke of Sarajevo: The Romance and Tragedy of Franz Ferdinand of Austria.* Boston: Little, Brown, 1984, p. 12.

CHAPTER 3: BUILDING A MODERN NATION

14. Eric Solsten and David E. McClave, eds., *Austria: A Country Study.* 2nd ed. Washington, DC: Federal Research Division, Library of Congress, 1994, p. 34.

15. McGuigan, *The Habsburgs*, p. 406.

16. John J. Putnam, "Those Eternal Austrians," *National Geographic,* April 1985, p. 426.

17. Solsten and McClave, *Austria: A Country Study*, p. 40.

18. Solsten and McClave, *Austria: A Country Study*, p. 45.

19. Sigurd Pacher, "Austria 1945–1995: The Economic Development of the Second Republic," Austrian Press and Information Service. www.austria.org/sep95/austria.htm.

20. Pacher, "Austria 1945–1995."

CHAPTER 4: INFRASTRUCTURE: MAKING THE MACHINERY HUM

21. Quoted in Timothy Heritage, "EU Partners Keep Up Pressure on Austria," AOL News (Reuters) Brussels, February 3, 2000.

22. Anti-Defamation League, "Joerg Haider: The Rise of an Austrian Extreme Rightist." www.adl.org/backgrounders/joerg_haider.html.

23. Quoted in Anti-Defamation League, "Joerg Haider."

24. Quoted in John O'Callaghan, "Austrian Minister Warns of 'Hot Mood' on Sanctions," AOL News (Reuters), London, June 9, 2000.

25. Stefan Tissot, interviews with the author, May 24 to 30, 2000.

26. Quoted in Jill Lawless, "Europeans Tighten Their Borders," AOL News (Associated Press), London, April 28, 2000.

27. Solsten and McClave, *Austria: A Country Study*, p. 133.

28. Tissot, interview.

29. Solsten and McClave, *Austria: A Country Study*, p. 119.

30. Solsten and McClave, *Austria: A Country Study*, p. 77.

31. Solsten and McClave, *Austria: A Country Study*, p. 78.

CHAPTER 5: A LEGACY OF CULTURAL EXCELLENCE

32. McGuigan, *The Habsburgs*, p. 207.

33. Geoffrey Hindley, Ed., *Larousse Encyclopedia of Music.* London: Hamlyn Publishing Group Ltd., 1971, p. 240.

34. Quoted in Midiworld, *Franz Joseph Haydn.* http://midiworld.com/haydn1.htm.

35. Quoted in McGuigan, *The Habsburgs*, p. 232.

36. Quoted in Peter T. White, "Vienna, City of Song," *National Geographic*, June 1968, p. 753.

37. White, "Vienna, City of Song," p. 751.

38. WebMuseum, Paris, "Gustav Klimt" http://sunsite.icm.edu.pl/wm/paint/auth/klimt/.

39. Sabina Wiedenhoeft, "A Comparative Study: Austrian Preservation," University of Vermont Historic Preservation Program. www.uvm.edu/~histpres/aust.html.

CHAPTER 6: FINDING A NATIONAL IDENTITY

40. Brook-Shepherd, *The Austrians*, p. 3.

41. Brook-Shepherd, *The Austrians*, p. xxiv.

42. Solsten and McClave, *Austria: A Country Study*, p. 79.

43. Solsten and McClave, *Austria: A Country Study*, p. 103.

44. Pelinka, *Austria: Out of the Shadow of the Past*, p. 232.

CHRONOLOGY

976
Babenbergs gain control of northeastern Austria.

1273
Rudolf I of Habsburg is chosen as Holy Roman emperor.

1358–1365
Reign of Rudolf IV

1438–1806
Archduchy of Austria is most important state in Holy Roman Empire.

1440
Friedrich III, duke of Styria, begins royal marriages that will give Habsburgs great power.

1519–1556
Reign of Charles V

1529
Turkish siege of Vienna

1556
Charles V abdicates and empire is divided into Spanish and Austrian branches. Charles's brother, Ferdinand I, becomes emperor of Austrian branch of the Habsburg dynasty.

1618–1648
Thirty Years' War: Ferdinand II attempts to wipe out Protestantism. Peace comes with signing of Treaty of Westphalia.

1683
Second Turkish siege of Vienna

1740–1748
War of the Austrian Succession; Maria Theresa consolidates empire.

1792–1835
Reign of Francis II

1806
Francis II renounces title of head of Holy Roman Empire and becomes emperor of Austria under name of Francis I.

1809
Metternich becomes chancellor.

1814–1815
Congress of Vienna; Austria recovers territories lost in wars with France.

1848
Fall of Metternich

1848–1916
Reign of Emperor Franz Joseph

1867
Creation of the dual Austro-Hungarian monarchy

1914
Assassination at Sarajevo of Crown Prince Francis Ferdinand starts World War I.

1914–1918
Austria-Hungary defeated in World War I; Emperor Karl I steps down.

1920
Democratic constitution adopted.

1938
Hitler invades Austria.

1944–1955
France, Great Britain, Russia, and the United States occupy Austria.

1970
Bruno Kreisky, head of the Socialist Party, is appointed chancellor.

1995
Austria joins European Union.

2000
Freedom Party joins governing coalition, and European Union levies sanctions against Austria.

GLOSSARY

Alemannic: Several German dialects spoken in areas of southwestern Germany, Alsace, and Switzerland settled by Alemanni tribes in the early fifth century A.D.

Baroque: A style of art and architecture characterized by much ornamentation and curved rather than straight lines.

Celts: Ancient people of central and western Europe.

coalition: A temporary alliance of factions, nations, etc., for some specific purpose.

duchy: The territory ruled by a duke or duchess.

fossil fuels: Fuels dug from the earth such as coal, petroleum, and natural gas.

gross domestic product (GDP): The total value of goods and services produced by the domestic economy during a given period, usually a year.

gross national product: The total value of a nation's GDP plus income received from abroad by residents, less payments remitted abroad to nonresidents.

infrastructure: The basic facilities of a community such as roads, schools, power plants, transportation, and communications.

mobilize: To become organized and ready, as for war.

nationalism: The belief that national interest and security are more important than international considerations.

nationalize: To transfer ownership or control of land, resources, or industries to the national government.

troubadours: Lyric poets and poet musicians of the Middle Ages. Also loosely used to mean any minstrel.

Suggestions for Further Reading

Books

John S. C. Abbott, *Austria: Its Rise and Power.* New York: Peter Fenelon Collier, 1892. An entertaining and interesting early history of Austria. However, sources and notes are sadly lacking. Direct quotes attributed to individuals may be more colorful than accurate.

George R. Marek, *The Eagles Die: Franz Joseph, Elisabeth, and Their Austria.* New York: Harper & Row, 1974. An in-depth and fascinating account of Emperor Franz Joseph's sixty-eight-year reign, with emphasis on the role played by his beautiful but flighty wife, Elisabeth. It is illustrated with many excellent photographs.

Sean Sheehan, *Austria.* Tarrytown, NY: Benchmark Books, 1995. Introduces the geography, history, economy, culture, and people of Austria.

Conrad Stein, *Vienna.* Danbury, CT: Childrens Press, 1999. This book explores modern life in Vienna and is well illustrated with color photos, drawings, and paintings.

Periodicals

Beverley M. Bowie, "The White Horses of Vienna," *National Geographic,* September 1958.

Mike W. Edwards, "The Danube: River of Many Nations, Many Names," *National Geographic,* October 1977.

David Roberts, "The Ice Man: Lone Voyager from the Copper Age," *National Geographic,* June 1993.

Websites

Austrian National Tourism Office. http://austria-tourism.at/header.html.

Austrian Press and Information Services. www.austria.org.

WORKS CONSULTED

BOOKS

Gordon Brook-Shepherd, *Archduke of Sarajevo: The Romance and Tragedy of Franz Ferdinand of Austria.* Boston: Little, Brown, 1984. The story of Franz Ferdinand, whose assassination by a Serbian nationalist in 1914 started World War I.

————, *The Austrians: A Thousand-Year Odyssey.* New York: Carrol & Graf, 1996. A well-researched and insightful book about the people of Austria over a thousand years of history.

Edward Crankshaw, *The Habsburgs: Portrait of a Dynasty.* New York: Viking Press, 1971. A beautifully written and illustrated journey through the Habsburg Dynasty.

Geoffrey Hindley, ed., *Larousse Encyclopedia of Music.* London: Hamlyn Publishing Group Ltd., 1971. A rather technical history of music in encyclopedic form which contains a wealth of photographs, drawings, paintings, and other illustrations.

Mark Honan, Austria. 2nd ed. Melbourne: Lonely Planet Publications, 1999. This travel guide contains a wealth of information on the history, climate, government, and education of Austria, as well as information on modern life, landmarks, and museums.

Dorothy Gies McGuigan, *The Habsburgs.* New York: Doubleday, 1966. This informative and entertaining book takes a close look at the personal lives of a royal family that made history for six centuries.

Anton Pelinka, *Austria: Out of the Shadow of the Past.* Boulder, CO: Westview Press, 1998. A scholarly and well-researched book on Austria's social and political structure since World War II, written by one of Austria's leading social scientists.

Eric Solsten and David E. McClave, eds., *Austria: A Country Study.* 2nd ed. Washington, DC: Federal Research Division, Library of Congress, 1994. A concise and objective review of the history, the military, society, politics, and economics of Austria.

PERIODICALS AND INTERVIEWS

Beverley M. Bowie, "Building a New Austria," *National Geographic,* February 1959.

——— , "Salzkammergut, Austria's Alpine Playground," *National Geographic,* August 1960.

George W. Long, "Outpost of Democracy," *National Geographic,* June 1951.

John J. Putnam, "Those Eternal Austrians," *National Geographic,* April 1985.

Stefan Tissot, interviews with the author, May 24 to 30, 2000.

Peter T. White, "Tirol, Austrian Province in the Clouds," *National Geographic,* July 1961.

——— , "Vienna, City of Song," *National Geographic,* June 1968.

INTERNET SOURCES

Anti-Defamation League, "Jean-Marie Le Pen: A Right-Wing Extremist and His Party." www.adl.org/international/lepen -1-introduction.html.

———, "Joerg Haider: The Rise of an Austrian Extreme Rightist." www.adl.org/backgrounders/joerg_haider.html.

"Austria to Insist on Limit on E. Europe Workers," AOL News, Brussels, May 10, 2000.

The Austria National Tourism Office, *The Spanish Riding School of Vienna.* http://austria-tourism.at/Hofreits chule/hofreitschule_e.html.

The Austria National Tourism Office. *The Vienna Giant Ferris Wheel.* www.austria-tourism.at/musts/riesenrad/.

"Austria in Court Threat over Alpine Lorry Traffic," AOL News, (Reuters), Luxembourg, June 26, 2000.

Encyclopedia of Austria. www.aeiou.at/aeiou.encyclop.m/ m0407464en.htm.

David Jagger, "Refugees and Racism in the New Germany," 1992, http://jinx.sistm.unsw.edu.au/~greenlft/1992/50/50p16.htm.

Julia Ferguson, "Chaos in Store on Key Alpine Route Due to Blockade," AOL News, Vienna, June 22, 2000.

——— , "Divers Start Hunt for Nazi Loot in Austrian Lake." AOL News (Reuters), Vienna, June 6, 2000.

Douglas Hamilton, "Homogenized Europe Still Far, Far Away," AOL News (Reuters), Brussels, June 28, 2000.

——— , "Wise Men Panel to Unblock EU-Austria Impasse," AOL News (Reuters), Brussels, June 27, 2000 .

Timothy Heritage, "Analysis—Austria Sees Hope of End to EU Isolation," AOL News (Reuters), Brussels, May 10, 2000.

——— , "EU Partners Keep Up Pressure on Austria," AOL News, (Reuters) Brussels, February 3, 2000.

Jill Lawless, "Europeans Tighten Their Borders," AOL News (Associated Press), London, April 28, 2000.

Midiworld, *Franz Joseph Haydn*, 1998. http://midiworld.com/haydn1.htm.

Mississippi State University, Historical Text Archive Austria-Hungary. www.msstate.edu/Archives/History/hungary/austria/contents.htm.

"Nordic EU States Say United Front Against Austria Vital," AOL News (Reuters), Skagen, Denmark, June 8, 2000.

John O'Callaghan, "Austrian Minister Warns of 'Hot Mood' on Sanctions," AOL News (Reuters), London, June 9, 2000.

Sigurd Pacher, "Austria 1945–1995: The Economic Development of the Second Republic," Austrian Press and Information Service. www. austria.org/sep95/austria.html.

Adriana Pontieri, "Protesters End Alpine Blockade but Threaten More," Schoenberg, Austria, AOL News (Reuters), June 24, 2000.

WebMuseum, Paris, "Gustav Klimt." http://sunsite.icm.edu.pl/wm/paint/auth/klimt.

Sabina Wiedenhoeft, "A Comparative Study: Austrian Preservation," University of Vermont Historic Preservation Program. http://www.uvm.edu/~histpres/aust.html.

INDEX

PICTURE CREDITS

ABOUT THE AUTHOR

Anne Ake edited an arts magazine for eight years, and with her daughter owned and published *Cool KidStuff*, a children's magazine. She has published several books and numerous articles on many topics from the arts to nature. As marketing manager of the Quality of Life Division of a navy base, Ms. Ake uses writing, desktop publishing, and graphic design skills to produce publications to publicize base leisure and recreational facilities and activities. She also edits and designs a newsletter for the state parks in the Northwest District of the Florida Park Service.